Congressional
Research
Service

Israel: Background and U.S. Relations

Jim Zanotti

Specialist in Middle Eastern Affairs

November 1, 2013

Congressional Research Service

7-5700

www.crs.gov

RL33476

CRS Report for Congress

Prepared for Members and Committees of Congress

Summary

Since Israel's founding in 1948, successive U.S. Presidents and many Members of Congress have demonstrated a commitment to Israel's security and to maintaining close U.S.-Israel defense, diplomatic, and economic cooperation. U.S. and Israeli leaders have developed close relations based on common perceptions of shared democratic values and religious affinities. U.S. policymakers often seek to determine how regional events and U.S. policy choices may affect Israel's security, and Congress provides active oversight of executive branch dealings with Israel and the broader Middle East. Some Members of Congress and some analysts criticize what they perceive as U.S. support for Israel without sufficient scrutiny of its actions. Israel is a leading recipient of U.S. foreign aid and is a frequent purchaser of major U.S. weapons systems. The United States and Israel maintain close security cooperation—predicated on a U.S. commitment to maintain Israel's "qualitative military edge" over other countries in its region. The two countries signed a free trade agreement in 1985, and the United States is Israel's largest trading partner. For more information, see CRS Report RL33222, *U.S. Foreign Aid to Israel*, by Jeremy M. Sharp.

Israel has many regional security concerns. Israeli leaders calling for urgent international action against Iran's nuclear program hint at the possibility of a unilateral military strike against Iran's nuclear facilities. In addition to concerns over Iran, Israel's perceptions of security around its borders have changed since early 2011 as several surrounding Arab countries—including Egypt and Syria—have experienced political upheaval. Israel has shown particular concern about threats from Hezbollah and other non-state groups in ungoverned or minimally governed areas in Syria, Lebanon, and Egypt's Sinai Peninsula, as well as from Hamas and other Palestinian militants in the Gaza Strip.

Israel's political impasse with the Palestinians on core issues in their longstanding conflict continues, though direct Israeli-Palestinian talks resumed in the summer of 2013. Since the end of the 1967 Arab-Israeli War, Israel has militarily occupied and administered the West Bank, with the Palestinian Authority exercising limited self-rule in some areas since 1995. Israeli settlement of that area, facilitated by successive Israeli governments, has resulted in a population of approximately 500,000 Israelis living in residential neighborhoods or settlements in the West Bank and East Jerusalem. These settlements are of disputed legality under international law. Israel considers all of Jerusalem to be the "eternal, undivided capital of Israel," but Palestinians claim a capital in East Jerusalem and some international actors advocate special political classification for the city or specific Muslim and Christian holy sites. Although Israel withdrew its permanent military presence and its settlers from the Gaza Strip in 2005, it still controls most access points and legal commerce to and from the territory.

Despite its unstable regional environment, Israel has developed a robust diversified economy and a vibrant democracy. Recent discoveries and exploitation of offshore natural gas raise the prospect of a more energy-independent future, while economic debates focus largely on cost-of-living and income and labor distribution issues. Israel's demographic profile has evolved in a way that appears to be affecting its political orientation. Along with secular and nationalist Jews from various ethnic backgrounds, Jewish ultra-Orthodox, Russian-speaking, and Arab citizens significantly influence societal debates. The government formed by Prime Minister Binyamin Netanyahu in March 2013 features a set of coalition partners that is different from the previous government, largely due to electoral gains on socioeconomic issues by new national leaders such as Yair Lapid and Naftali Bennett.

Contents

Figures

Tables

Appendixes

Contacts

Introduction

U.S.-Israel defense, diplomatic, and economic cooperation has been close for decades. U.S. policymakers often consider Israel's security as they make policy choices in the region. Israel has relied on U.S. support for its defense posture, despite reported private and sometimes public disagreements between U.S. and Israeli officials on how to respond to and prioritize various security challenges. Congress provides active oversight of the executive branch's dealings with Israel. Some Members of Congress oppose what they perceive as U.S. support of Israel without sufficient scrutiny of Israel's actions. Other Members of Congress have criticized actions by the Obama Administration and previous U.S. Administrations for being insufficiently supportive of Israel, and occasionally have authorized and appropriated funding for programs benefitting Israel at a level exceeding that requested by the executive branch.

U.S. approaches to a number of challenges in the Middle East have implications for Israel. For several years now, Israeli leaders have described Iran and its reported pursuit of a nuclear weapons capability as an imminent threat to Israeli security. Israeli officials have claimed that their window of opportunity to act on their own to delay, halt, or reverse Iranian progress toward a nuclear weapons capability is closing. Consequently, they have sought increasingly stringent measures from the international community intended to compel Iran to negotiate limitations that ensure that its nuclear program is exclusively for peaceful purposes. Within this context, Israeli leaders have publicly hinted that absent a clear resolution of Iran's nuclear activity to their satisfaction, they may order the Israeli military to strike Iranian nuclear facilities.

Many Israeli officials also are concerned with the rise of Islamist political movements and threats posed by violent jihadist terrorist groups emanating from ongoing regional political turmoil. Israel has few means of influencing political outcomes in Egypt, Syria, Lebanon, or Jordan, but developments in those states may significantly affect Israeli security. Syria's civil war is posing increasing risk to Israel, leading to limited Israeli military action and raising the possibility of more overt conflict involving the Asad regime and/or Hezbollah—which is directly intervening in support of the regime. Instability in Egypt's Sinai Peninsula has already been used by militant groups—probably including Al Qaeda-style Palestinian cells—for attacks on Israeli targets. At the same time, many large and small Israeli population centers remain threatened by rocket fire from Hamas and other terrorist groups in Gaza.

Israel's disputes continue with the Palestine Liberation Organization (PLO) over the terms of a potential peace agreement on issues including security parameters, borders, Jewish settlements, water rights, Palestinian refugees, and the status of Jerusalem. Partly as a result of active U.S. efforts, Israel and the PLO restarted direct negotiations in the summer of 2013, but the talks' prospects remain uncertain. Failure to make progress could have a number of regional and global implications, including a possible return by the PLO to a strategy of seeking greater international recognition of Palestinian statehood.

Country Background

Historical Overview[1]

The start of a quest for a modern Jewish homeland can be traced to the publication of Theodor Herzl's *The Jewish State* in 1896. Herzl was inspired by the concept of nationalism that had become popular among various European peoples in the 19th century, and was also motivated by his perception of European anti-Semitism. The following year, Herzl described his vision at the first Zionist Congress, which encouraged Jewish settlement in Palestine, the territory that had included the Biblical home of the Jews but was then part of the Ottoman Empire. During World War I, the British government issued the Balfour Declaration in 1917, supporting the "establishment in Palestine of a national home for the Jewish people." Palestine became a British Mandate after the war and British officials simultaneously encouraged the national aspirations of the Arab majority in Palestine for eventual self-determination, insisting that its promises to Jews and Arabs did not conflict. Jews immigrated to Palestine in ever greater numbers during the Mandate period, and tension between Arabs and Jews and between each group and the British increased, leading to periodic clashes. Following World War II, the plight of Jewish survivors of the Holocaust gave the demand for a Jewish home added poignancy and urgency, while Arabs across the Middle East simultaneously demanded self-determination and independence from European colonial powers.

In 1947, the United Nations General Assembly developed a partition plan (Resolution 181) to divide Palestine into Jewish and Arab states, proposing U.N. trusteeship for Jerusalem and some surrounding areas. The leadership of the Jewish Yishuv (or polity) welcomed the plan because of the legitimacy they asserted that it conferred on the Jews' claims in Palestine despite their small numbers, while the Palestinian Arab leadership and the League of Arab States (Arab League) rejected the plan, insisting both that the specific partition proposed and the entire concept of partition were unfair given Palestine's Arab majority. Debate on this question prefigured current debate about whether it is possible to have a state that both provides a secure Jewish homeland and is governed in accordance with democratic values and the principle of self-determination.

After several months of civil conflict between Jews and Arabs, Britain officially ended its Mandate on May 14, 1948, at which point the state of Israel proclaimed its independence and was immediately invaded by Arab armies. During and after the conflict, roughly 700,000 Palestinians were driven or fled from their homes, an occurrence Palestinians call the *nakba* ("catastrophe").[2] Many became internationally designated refugees after ending up either in areas of Mandate-era Palestine controlled by Jordan (the West Bank) or Egypt (the Gaza Strip), or in nearby Arab states. Palestinians remaining in Israel became Israeli citizens.

The conflict ended with armistice agreements between Israel and its neighboring Arab states: Egypt, Jordan, Lebanon, and Syria. The territory controlled by Israel within these 1949-1950 armistice lines is roughly the size of New Jersey. Israel engaged in further armed conflict with some or all of its neighbors in 1956, 1967, 1973, and 1982. Since the late 1960s, Israel has also dealt with the threat of Palestinian nationalist and (later) Islamist terrorism. In 1979, Israel

---

[1] For more, see Howard M. Sachar, *A History of Israel: From the Rise of Zionism to Our Time*, New York: Knopf, 1996.

[2] CRS Report RL34074, *The Palestinians: Background and U.S. Relations*, by Jim Zanotti.

concluded a peace treaty with Egypt, followed in 1994 by a peace treaty with Jordan, thus making another multi-front war less likely. However, as discussed throughout the report, major security challenges persist from Iran and groups allied with it. Additionally, developments in Arab states and in the ongoing Israeli-Palestinian conflict further complicate Israel's regional position.

Demographic and Political Changes

Israel's demographic profile has evolved in a way that appears to be affecting its political orientation and societal debates. In the first decades following its founding, Israeli society was dominated by secular Ashkenazi Jews from Eastern Europe who constituted the large majority of 19th and early 20th century Zionist immigrants. Many leaders from these immigrant communities sought to build a country dedicated to Western liberal and communitarian values. The 1977 electoral victory of Menachem Begin's Likud party helped boost the influence of previously marginalized groups, particularly Mizrahi (Eastern) Jews who had largely immigrated to Israel from Arab countries and Iran. Subsequently other distinct groups, such as Haredim (ultra-Orthodox) from communities that predated Zionist immigration, and Russian-speaking Israelis who emigrated from the former Soviet Union in the 1990s,[3] have increased their numbers—and consequently their influence—in Israeli society. Israel also faces considerable estrangement between its Jewish and Arab citizens. Arabs comprise more than 20% of the population, and Islamist movements are increasingly popular in some Arab Israeli communities.

Political parties linked to recently expanded segments of Jewish Israeli society tend to favor the right side of the Israeli political spectrum currently led by Binyamin Netanyahu and Likud. At the same time, general trends show that support for traditionally left-leaning Zionist parties such as Labor has decreased. Issues regarding religiosity in the public sphere and secular consternation at subsidies and widespread exemptions from military service for Haredim (many of whom engage in religious study as an alternative to employment) have driven recent political debate. Military service remains compulsory for most Jewish Israeli young men and women.

Many analysts believe that these changes partly explain why Israel's current Jewish population is "more nationalistic, religiously conservative, and hawkish on foreign policy and security affairs than that of even a generation ago."[4] These trends' likely long-term effects on Israel's internal cohesion and its ties with the United States and other international actors are unclear.

---

[3] Most of these Russian-speaking emigrants are Ashkenazi and tend to be secular, but are generally more sympathetic with right-leaning parties than with the old Ashkenazi elite.

[4] Haim Malka, *Crossroads: The Future of the U.S.-Israel Strategic Partnership*, Washington, DC: Center for Strategic and International Studies, 2011, p. 19.

Figure 1. Map of Israel

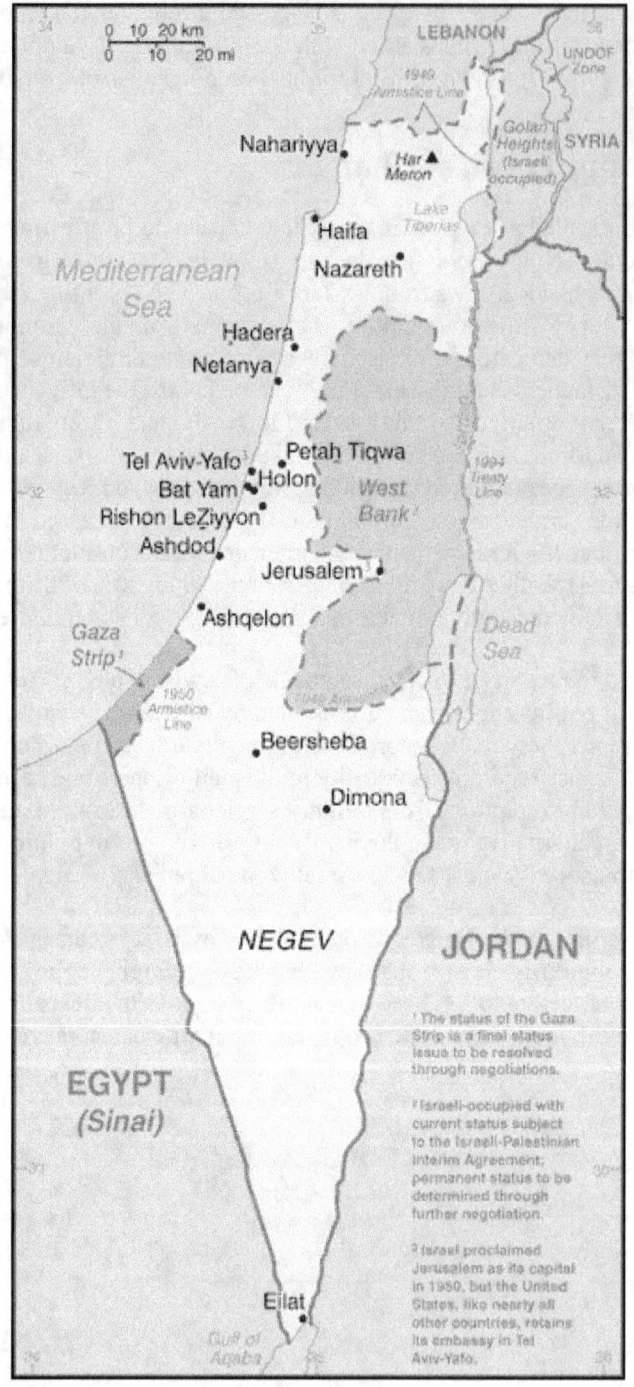

Source: CIA, *The World Factbook.*

Government and Politics

Overview

Israel is a parliamentary democracy in which the prime minister is head of government and the president is a largely ceremonial head of state. The unicameral parliament (the Knesset) elects a president for a seven-year term. Israel does not have a written constitution. Instead, 11 Basic Laws lay down the rules of government and enumerate fundamental rights. Israel has an independent judiciary, with a system of magistrates' courts and district courts headed by a Supreme Court.

The political spectrum is highly fragmented, with small parties exercising disproportionate power due to the low vote threshold (2%) for entry into the Knesset, and larger parties seeking small party support to form and maintain coalition governments. Since Israel's founding, the average lifespan of an Israeli government has been about 23 months. In recent years, however, the Knesset has somewhat tightened the conditions for bringing down a government.

Primer on Israeli Electoral Process and Government-Building[5]

Elections to Israel's 120-seat Knesset are direct, secret, and proportional based on a party list system, with the entire country constituting a single electoral district. All Israeli citizens age 18 and older may vote. Turnout in elections since 2001 has ranged between 62-67% of registered voters (before that it generally ranged between 77-80%)[6]. Elections must be held at least every four years, but are often held earlier due to difficulties in holding coalitions together. A Central Elections Committee is responsible for conducting and supervising the elections. The committee includes representatives from parties in the current Knesset and is headed by a Supreme Court justice.

National laws provide parameters for candidate eligibility, general elections, and party primaries—including specific conditions and limitations on campaign contributions and public financing for parties.[7] Since 2007, a "cooling-off law" requires that senior Israeli military officers wait at least three years before entering civilian politics.[8]

---

[5] Much of the information for this textbox comes from Israel's Ministry of Foreign Affairs website, "Elections in Israel - February 2009," February 10, 2009.

[6] International Institute for Democracy and Electoral Assistance, "Voter turnout data for Israel," October 5, 2011; Alistair Lyon, "Netanyahu claims election win despite losses," *Reuters*, January 22, 2013.

[7] For additional details on Israel's campaign finance laws, see Ruth Levush, "Campaign Finance: Israel," Law Library of Congress, July 25, 2012.

[8] The law, sponsored by Likud's Yuval Steinitz, was reportedly intended to counter Israeli military officers' cultivation of civilian political connections and influence in anticipation of their possible career transitions. Some reports criticized the law's failure to address the use of influence by civilian politicians to prepare for private sector career transitions. Nehemia Shtrasler, "The Bottom Line / Lawmakers don't need to cool off too?" *Ha'aretz*, May 16, 2007.

Following elections, the task of forming a government is given by Israel's president to the Knesset member he/she believes has the best chance to form a government as prime minister. The would-be prime minister has 28 days to assemble a majority coalition, and the president can extend this period for an additional 14 days. The government and its ministers are installed following a vote of confidence by at least 61 Knesset members. Thereafter, the ministers determine the government's course of action on domestic issues, while military and national security action are directed through a "security cabinet" (formally known as the Ministerial Committee on Defense) consisting of a group of key ministers—some whose membership is set by law, others who are appointed by the prime minister—who number no more than half of all cabinet ministers.[9]

For the first 30 years of Israel's existence (1948-1977), the social democratic Mapai/Labor movement—led by a founding Ashkenazi Zionist elite of Eastern European descent—dominated Israeli governing coalitions. As questions regarding the future of territories that Israel's military occupied during the 1967 Arab-Israeli War became increasingly central to political life, the nationalist Likud party and its prominent prime ministers Menachem Begin and Yitzhak Shamir helped drive the political agenda over the following 15 years. Although Labor under Yitzhak Rabin later initiated the Oslo peace process with the Palestinians, its political momentum was slowed and reversed after Rabin's assassination in 1995. Despite Labor's setbacks, its warnings regarding the demographic challenge that high Arab birth rates could eventually present to continued Israeli political control over Palestinians, under the rubric of maintaining both a Jewish and a democratic state, gained traction among many Israelis. In this context, Prime Minister Ariel Sharon, a longtime champion of the Israeli right and settlement movement, split from Likud and established Kadima as a more centrist alternative in 2005. Elections in February 2009 were a divided affair, with Tzipi Livni's Kadima winning the most Knesset seats but Netanyahu's Likud leading the coalition because of an overall advantage for right-of-center parties. For more recent developments, see "2013 Elections and Current Government" below.

Table 1. Israeli Security Cabinet Members

Member	Party	Ministerial Position(s)	Previous Knesset Terms
Binyamin Netanyahu	Likud	Prime Minister	7
		Minister of Foreign Affairs	
		Minister of Public Diplomacy and Diaspora Affairs	
Moshe Ya'alon	Likud	Minister of Defense	1
Yair Lapid	Yesh Atid	Minister of Finance	0
Naftali Bennett	Ha'bayit Ha'Yehudi	Minister of Economy and Trade	0
		Minister of Religious Affairs	
Tzipi Livni	Ha'tnua	Minister of Justice	4
Yitzhak Aharonovich	Yisrael Beiteinu	Minister of Public Security	2

---

[9] According to a one media report, "Under Israeli law, war must be approved by the full cabinet. But the security cabinet, whose secrecy is better enforced, can green-light more limited military 'missions'. Making that distinction depends on whether Israel's intelligence chiefs anticipate an escalation into protracted conflict." Dan Williams, "Netanyahu's new security cabinet may hesitate on any Iran war," *Reuters*, March 19, 2013. Historically, Israeli prime ministers (including Netanyahu) have appeared to prefer convening the smaller forum for consultative purposes when convening the larger one is not legally required. See, e.g., Eli Lake, "Meet the Israeli 'Octet' That Would Decide an Iran Attack," *Daily Beast*, March 9, 2012. For a primer on and historical overview of Israel's national security decisionmaking process by a former Israeli security official, see Charles D. Freilich, *Zion's Dilemmas: How Israel Makes National Security Policy*, Ithaca, New York: Cornell University, 2012. For a more concise version of the same subject matter, see Charles D. Freilich, "National Security Decision-Making in Israel: Improving the Process," *Middle East Journal*, vol. 67, no. 2, spring 2013.

Member	Party	Ministerial Position(s)	Previous Knesset Terms
Gilad Erdan	Likud	Minister of Communications	3
		Minister of Home Front Defense	

Note: Avigdor Lieberman of Yisrael Beiteinu (four previous Knesset terms) is expected to join the security cabinet if he returns as foreign minister following his criminal trial. Ben Caspit, "The Trial of Avigdor Liberman," *Al-Monitor Israel Pulse*, May 31, 2013.

2013 Elections and Current Government

The current Israeli coalition government was sworn in on March 18, 2013, following elections that took place on January 22, 2013. The right-of-center[10] "Likud Beiteinu" list,[11] featuring Prime Minister Binyamin Netanyahu's Likud party and Yisrael Beiteinu (Israel Is Our Home), has the most seats (31) in the 120-seat Knesset (parliament), but 11 fewer than its constituent parties had in the previous Knesset. After a surprisingly strong showing in January's elections, the newly formed, centrist Yesh Atid (There Is a Future), led by former journalist Yair Lapid,[12] has the second-largest Knesset representation (19 seats). Lapid and Naftali Bennett[13] of the pro-settler party Ha'bayit Ha'Yehudi agreed to join the government with Likud Beiteinu and the centrist Ha'tnua party after reportedly agreeing on basic parameters with Netanyahu over plans to remove the general exemption from mandatory conscription for young ultra-Orthodox men. Netanyahu also reportedly agreed in principle to raise the electoral threshold for political parties seeking to enter the Knesset from 2% to 4%. Shelly Yachimovich formally leads the opposition as head of its largest party, Labor. Other elements of the opposition include the ultra-Orthodox parties Shas and United Torah Judaism. For a breakdown of the electoral lists with Knesset seats, see **Appendix B**.

---

[10] In Israel, the left-right spectrum has been traditionally defined by parties' positions on the Israeli-Palestinian conflict/peace process, though the spectrum also has some validity in describing differences on economic and social issues.

[11] Under Israeli electoral law, lists for Knesset elections may consist of one party or multiple parties running jointly.

[12] For a profile of Lapid, see Raffi Berg, "Profile: Yair Lapid, Israel's Yesh Atid party leader," *BBC News*, March 14, 2013.

[13] Bennett, who is routinely described as a young, charismatic leader helping remake his party, is also a multimillionaire former businessman and was a former chief of staff to Netanyahu during his time as opposition leader in 2006-2008 before the two reportedly had a falling out of sorts. Bennett favors Israeli annexation of a large part of the West Bank. Jodi Rudoren, "Dynamic Former Netanyahu Aide Shifts Israeli Campaign Rightward," *New York Times*, December 26, 2012.

Figure 2. Israeli Knesset

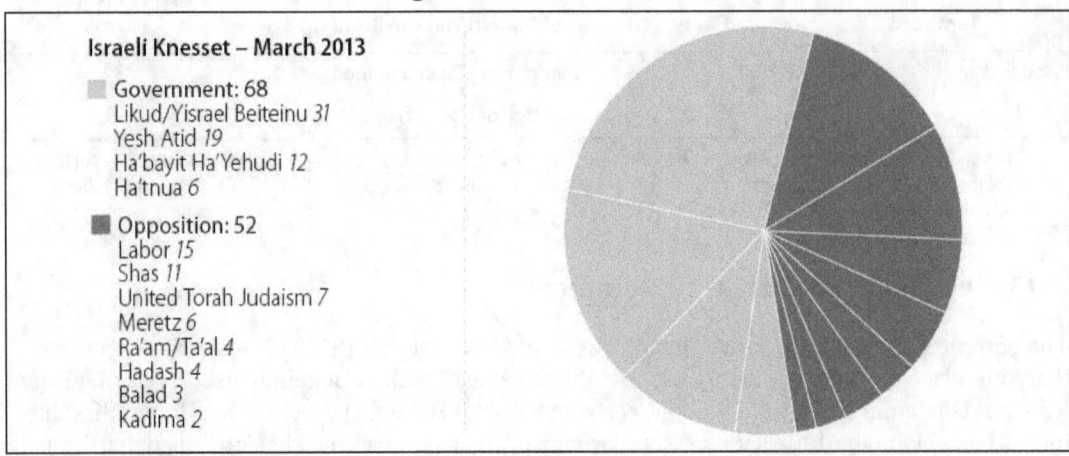

Israeli Knesset – March 2013

Government: 68
Likud/Yisrael Beiteinu *31*
Yesh Atid *19*
Ha'bayit Ha'Yehudi *12*
Ha'tnua *6*

Opposition: 52
Labor *15*
Shas *11*
United Torah Judaism *7*
Meretz *6*
Ra'am/Ta'al *4*
Hadash *4*
Balad *3*
Kadima *2*

There has been much speculation over the implications of the January elections' outcome for the future of Israel's political leadership. It is possible that the coalition could collapse over disagreements on Palestinian or socioeconomic issues and trigger another round of elections before they would be required in late 2017.[14] However, initial speculation that Yair Lapid's rise might represent a fundamental reorientation of Israeli politics in favor of his party or centrist parties in general has largely subsided. Public opinion polls since mid-2013 have revealed negative approval ratings for Lapid,[15] who as finance minister became a leading face of unpopular austerity measures (referenced below) for Israel's 2013-2014 budget.

At the same time, internal struggles within Netanyahu's Likud party may affect its future leadership and direction. Tensions reportedly exist between established party veterans and younger politicians who advocate more nationalistic positions and confrontational tactics on Palestinian and other civil society issues. Likud's diminished Knesset and cabinet representation relative to the previous (2009-2013) government appears to have exacerbated these tensions.

According to many observers, the January 2013 elections largely hinged on domestic socioeconomic issues, a departure from the Palestinian issue's traditional predominance in Israeli political discourse. Despite consistent economic growth and Israel's stable fiscal position, these issues drove large, non-violent domestic protests in the summer of 2011.[16] Although the government agreed in May 2013 on a 2013-2014 budget that will incorporate spending cuts and tax increases in order to control Israel's fiscal deficit, cost-of-living and income distribution issues continue to generate contention. Other matters that garner significant domestic attention include the influence of ultra-Orthodox Jewish communities on gender roles in the public sphere, as well as tensions between avowed Jewish nationalist elements of society and Palestinians (including Arab Israelis), non-Jewish religious groups, and some other Jewish Israelis.[17] U.S. officials have expressed concern over these dynamics.[18]

---

[14] See, e.g., Jeffrey Heller, "Israel coalition wobbles over proposed military service law," *Reuters*, May 27, 2013.

[15] Yossi Verter, "Coalition roundup: Lapid's losing ground, Deri can't get a break, and Netanyahu's rising in the poll thanks to Iran," *haaretz.com*, October 19, 2013.

[16] Various factors—including Israel's communitarian heritage, its tradition of vigorous public debate, and the consequences of deregulation for a system characterized by some as "crony capitalism"—may have contributed to the protests.

[17] Such tensions include "price tag" attacks and vandalism in retaliation for government action or anticipated action (continued...)

Economy

In General

Israel has an advanced industrial, market economy in which the government plays a substantial role. Despite limited natural resources, the agricultural and industrial sectors are well developed. The engine of the economy is an advanced high-tech sector, including aviation, communications, computer-aided design and manufactures, medical electronics, and fiber optics. Israel still benefits from loans, contributions, and capital investments from the Jewish diaspora, but its economic strength has lessened its dependence on external financing.

Israel's economy appears to be experiencing a moderate slowdown after years of sustained, robust growth (nearly 5% from 2010 to 2011, for example). The slowdown seems to be largely due to second-order effects from down economies in Israel's largest export markets in Europe and North America. According to the Economist Intelligence Unit, Israel's growth in real GDP, estimated at 3.3% for 2012, is forecast to remain at or just above 3% in 2013 and 2014.[19] In subsequent years, however, the central bank's relatively expansionary monetary policy, continued export diversification, and anticipated new income from recently discovered offshore natural gas deposits (as discussed below) are expected to return economic growth to 4-6%.[20]

When Prime Minister Netanyahu was finance minister in the early 2000s, the government attempted to liberalize the economy by controlling government spending, reducing taxes, and privatizing state enterprises. The chronic budget deficit decreased, while the country's international credit rating was raised, enabling a drop in interest rates. However, Netanyahu's critics suggest that cuts in social spending widened income inequality and shrank the Israeli middle class.[21] A May 2013 Organisation for Economic Co-operation and Development (OECD) report stated that Israel has the highest poverty rate of any OECD country (slightly more than 20%) and the fifth-highest level of income inequality.[22]

(...continued)

limiting settlements or countering outposts unsanctioned by Israeli law. Yossi Melman, "A price tag for Jewish terror," *Jerusalem Report*, May 6, 2013.

[18] Barak Ravid, "Clinton warns of Israel's eroding democratic values," *Ha'aretz*, December 5, 2011.

[19] Economist Intelligence Unit, *Country Report: Israel*, generated October 30, 2013.

[20] Ibid.

[21] "How Netanyahu Went from Idealism to Pragmatism on Economic Policy" Knowledge@Wharton Blog, October 10, 2012.

[22] OECD, "Crisis squeezes income and puts pressure on inequality and poverty," May 15, 2013.

Table 2. Basic Facts

Population	7.70 million (2013 est.) (includes an estimated 325,500 settlers in the West Bank (2011 est.), 186,929 in East Jerusalem (2010 est.), and 18,700 in the Golan Heights (2011 est.))
Jews	75.4%
Arabs	20.5% (84.1% Muslim, 8.1% Druze, 7.8% Christian) (2011 est.)
Real Gross Domestic Product growth rate	3.0% (2013 est.)
GDP per capita (at purchasing power parity)	$33,441 (2013 est.)
Unemployment rate	6.8% (2013 est.)
Population below poverty line	23.6% (2007 est.)
Inflation rate	2.0% (2013 est.)
Defense spending as % of GDP	5.3% (2013 proj.)
Budget deficit as % of GDP	3.5% (2013 est.)
Public Debt as % of GDP	73.6% (2012 est.)
Foreign exchange and gold reserves	$75.9 billion (2012 est.)
Current account (Trade) surplus as % of GDP	1.8% (2013 est.)
Exports	$61.4 billion (2012 est.)
Export commodities	machinery and equipment, software, cut diamonds, agricultural products, chemicals, textile and apparel
Export partners	U.S. 27.8%, Hong Kong 7.7%, United Kingdom 5.7%, Belgium 4.6%, China 4.3% (2012 est.)
Imports	$71.4 billion (2012 est.)
Import commodities	raw materials, military equipment, investment goods, rough diamonds, fuels, grain, consumer goods
Import partners	U.S. 12.9%, China 7.3%, Germany 6.3%, Switzerland 5.5%, Belgium 4.8% (2012 est.)

Sources: Central Intelligence Agency, *The World Factbook*; Economist Intelligence Unit; Israel Central Bureau of Statistics, *Jane's Defence Procurement Budgets*.

Natural Gas Resources and Export Possibilities[23]

Natural gas production from Israel's first major offshore field, Tamar, began flowing in March 2013, ushering in a new era of Israel as an energy producer and possibly an exporter. Since Egypt cut its natural gas exports to Israel in 2012, the Israeli government has been pushing the companies involved in Tamar to begin production as quickly as possible to make up the

---

[23] This section was authored by Michael Ratner, Specialist in Energy Policy. See also archived CRS Report R41618, *Israel's Offshore Natural Gas Discoveries Enhance Its Economic and Energy Outlook*, by Michael Ratner.

shortfall.[24] With a second, larger offshore natural gas field, Leviathan,[25] still under development, Israel is facing questions of how to best utilize its natural gas resources.

Prior to the recent offshore natural gas discoveries, Israel had about 16 years' worth of natural gas at its production levels. If only half the estimated natural gas resources from the new discoveries is produced and consumed at 2012 levels, Israel would have almost a 200-year supply of natural gas.[26] At 2011 levels, Israel would have about a 100-year supply.[27] It is too early to know the rate of natural gas recovery from all the new fields or if other discoveries will be made, but it is highly likely that Israel's energy mix will move toward natural gas by the end of the decade. Initial production from Leviathan is projected to take place in 2016.[28] According to Noble Energy, the U.S.-based company that is responsible for Leviathan and Tamar, Tamar is expected to reach a capacity of almost one billion cubic feet per day (bcf/d), with a possible expansion to 1.5 bcf/d by 2015, which represents approximately six times the rate of Israeli consumption in 2012 (0.25 bcf/d). In 2013, Israel's Natural Gas Authority projects consumption to almost triple and to be met exclusively from domestic sources, mainly the Tamar field.[29]

Whether Israel will become an exporter of natural gas is yet to be determined. If the resource estimates are correct, the new fields would give Israel the resources to become an exporter. Future export options include sending natural gas by pipeline to Jordan and other neighbors, and/or producing liquefied natural gas (LNG) that can be exported more broadly. However, a number of factors raise doubts about the viability of exports: growing domestic demand (possibly driven by new uses for natural gas), the expense of liquefying the natural gas for transport, competitive projects in other countries, and the politics of pipeline exports. Overarching regional political and security issues also appear to be factors.[30]

Additionally, if more natural gas and possibly oil resources are to be developed, Israel's government will probably need to assuage energy industry concerns about the changing nature of its regulatory regime. The government's announcement in June 2013 that it plans to keep more natural gas than expected (60%) for domestic consumption—leaving only 40% for exports—may not bode well for future development.[31] Industry had apparently been hoping that at least 50% of the natural gas would be available for export, including through the possible involvement of

---

[24] Production has also been increased at some smaller fields.

[25] The Leviathan field, located off Israel's northern coast, has an estimated resource base of 17 trillion cubic feet (tcf) of natural gas. Tamar holds approximately 8.4 tcf. Both fields were discovered by U.S.-based company Noble Energy. Rodney Cook, Senior Vice President - International, *Noble Energy Analyst Conference Presentation*, Noble Energy, December 6, 2012, p. 17. Since January 2009, Noble Energy has made six natural gas discoveries (counting Tamar and Leviathan) with a total estimated 35 tcf of natural gas resources. Ibid., p. 5.

[26] When natural gas or oil is referred to as a resource, it implies that the natural gas or oil is technically recoverable, but may not be economical to produce. This is a less certain classification than a proved reserve, which means the natural gas or oil can be produced with existing technology and under current market conditions.

[27] Israel's natural gas consumption in 2011 is probably a more realistic depiction of the country's current annual demand, as 2012 saw a dramatic decline in Israeli natural gas consumption because of the stoppage of exports by Egypt.

[28] Cook, op. cit., p. 17.

[29] Email from Israel's Natural Gas Authority with the data showing these projections, June 30, 2013.

[30] Tia Goldenberg, "Israel faces geopolitical tangle with natural gas," *Daily Star* (Lebanon), March 29, 2013. See also James Stocker, "No EEZ Solution: The Politics of Oil and Gas in the Eastern Mediterranean," *Middle East Journal*, vol. 66, no. 4 (autumn 2012), pp. 579-597.

[31] "Israel's top court gives government 15 days to respond to appeal against gas exports," *Platts*, June 25, 2013, online.

Woodside, an Australian company. Noble Energy and its partners were hoping to bring Woodside into the project, as it has experience with LNG (in Australia) that Noble Energy and its partners do not have. However, Woodside has delayed a possible decision to buy into the Leviathan project. In October, one of Woodside's apparent concerns was alleviated when Israel's Supreme Court rejected a lawsuit brought by various environmental organizations to halt or delay the government's export plans.[32]

Noble Energy and its Israeli partners are exploring the possibility of building a liquefaction facility, possibly in Cyprus, to utilize any natural gas discovered there for exports to Europe and Asia. It remains too early to determine the feasibility of such a project. Cyprus, which is a European Union member and currently does not consume any natural gas in its economy, has embarked on a significant, long-term program to develop necessary infrastructure to do so. In late June 2013, Cyprus and a U.S.-Israeli partnership (with Noble Energy as one of the partners and responsible for the drilling) signed a memorandum of understanding to build natural gas facilities for both domestic consumption and export. A cost effective way for both countries to export their natural gas could be for Israel to pipe its exportable gas to Cyprus. The Israeli gas and any exportable Cypriot natural gas could then be liquefied and shipped.

Israel's Security Concerns

General Threat Perceptions

A leading Israeli commentator has written, "The region is in the throes of major historic change. For Israel, there are real dangers and significant opportunities."[33] It is largely unclear how shifts in regional order and various asymmetric threats may affect Israel's capabilities to project military strength, deter attack, and defend its population and strategically important sites, even as Israel's regional conventional military superiority persists and may even continue to grow.

Some unconventional threats to Israel are generally seen to have been reduced because of factors such as heightened security measures vis-à-vis Palestinians; missile defense systems; and reported cyberwarfare capabilities. From a physical security standpoint, Israel is nearing completion of a national border fence network of steel barricades (accompanied by watch towers, patrol roads, intelligence centers and military brigades), which is presumably designed to minimize militant infiltration, illegal immigration, and smuggling from Egypt, Syria, Lebanon, and even Jordan.[34]

Debate continues over the urgency of a political resolution to Israel's disputes with the Palestinians, as well as the potential regional and international consequences—including possibly increased "isolation"—if no resolution occurs. Analysts also have varying views regarding the extent to which Israel maintains deterrence over non-state militant groups such as Hamas and Hezbollah.

---

[32] Hila Raz, "Supreme Court rejects petition to halt Israel's natural gas exports," *haaretz.com*, October 21, 2013.

[33] Leslie Susser, "Strategic dilemmas," *Jerusalem Report*, May 20, 2013.

[34] William Booth, "With Golan fence, Israel closer to surrounding itself with barriers," *Washington Post*, June 6, 2013.

Challenges from Iran and Arab Neighbors

Over the nearly 40 years since the last major Arab-Israeli War in 1973, Israel has relied on the following three advantages—all either explicitly or implicitly backed by the United States—to remove or minimize potential threats to its security and existence:

- Overwhelming conventional military superiority;

- Formally ambiguous but universally presumed regional nuclear weapons exclusivity;[35] and

- De jure or de facto arrangements or relations with the authoritarian leaders of its Arab state neighbors aimed at preventing interstate conflict.

Although, as stated above, Israel's conventional military advantages are clear, the other two advantages listed above could face threats from the following strategic challenges. They are therefore subjects of serious concern among Israelis:

- ***Iranian Nuclear Challenge.*** Iran's possible achievement of a nuclear weapons capability, either for direct use or to exercise indirect but decisive influence on the region, could worsen security dilemmas. Israeli leaders have asserted that even if Iran does not use, intend to use, or even manufacture a nuclear weapon, its mere capacity to do so will increase its deterrence by raising the potential costs Israel and others would incur by acting against it or its allies (i.e., Hezbollah and various Palestinian militant groups). The resulting intimidation could lead Arab Gulf states in proximity to Iran to adopt more quiescent or pro-Iranian policies or to pursue nuclear capabilities of their own. In turn, this could open the way for increased Iranian influence and/or nuclear proliferation throughout the region. Prime Minister Netanyahu reportedly fears that such intimidation could lead to a "mass exodus of Jews from an Israel under nuclear threat, weakening the state and compromising the Zionist dream."[36]

- ***Islamist-Led or -Influenced Arab States.*** Sunni Islamist-led or -influenced Arab states may actively or tacitly support increased political pressure against Israel, particularly on the Palestinian issue, and/or increased military mobilization at or near its borders. Anti-Israel sentiments are widespread in other Middle Eastern states. These sentiments are not exclusive to Islamists, but country-specific and region-wide Islamist narratives, political constructs, and media platforms offer possible channels for coordinating their impact. This trend is reflected in a number of Arab countries where political change and turmoil has empowered Islamist movements and militias. However, the Egyptian military's ouster of Muslim Brotherhood figure Muhammad Morsi as president in July 2013 appears to have countered the trend somewhat.

- ***Instability and Terrorism from Ungoverned Spaces.*** Ungoverned or minimally governed spaces are proliferating near Israel's borders in Syria, Lebanon, Egypt's

---

[35] Israel is not a party to the Nuclear Non-Proliferation Treaty (NPT) and maintains a policy of "nuclear opacity" or *amimut*. A consensus among media and analysts' reports is that Israel possesses an arsenal of 80 to 200 nuclear weapons. See, e.g., Timothy McDonnell, "Nuclear pursuits: Non-P-5 nuclear-armed states, 2013," *Bulletin of the Atomic Scientists*, vol. 69(1), 2013.

[36] Leslie Susser, "Spy vs. Spy," *Jerusalem Report*, March 26, 2012.

Sinai Peninsula, and Libya. These areas attract or could attract terrorists, weapons traffickers, criminal networks, refugees, and migrants, and contribute to trends that appear to threaten Israeli security.[37] Such concerns appear to be motivating the construction of border fences with accompanying security measures, as mentioned above.[38]

Israeli planners and decision makers have scrambled to determine how to properly address these potential threats by recalibrating resource allocations, military postures, and regional and international political activities.

Iran[39]

For several years, Israeli leaders have described Iran and its reported pursuit of a nuclear weapons capability as an imminent threat to Israeli security. Israeli officials have claimed that their window of opportunity to act on their own to delay, halt, or reverse Iranian progress toward a nuclear weapons capability is closing. They have sought increasingly stringent measures from the international community to compel Iran to accept limitations to ensure that its nuclear program is exclusively for peaceful purposes. In remarks made prior to an October 2013 meeting in Rome with Secretary of State John Kerry, Netanyahu laid out Israel's four demands regarding Iran's nuclear program:

> Iran must not have a nuclear weapons capability, which means that they shouldn't have centrifuges for enrichment. They shouldn't have a plutonium heavy water plant which is used only for nuclear weapons.[40] They should get rid of the amassed fissile material. And they shouldn't have underground nuclear facilities, underground for one reason—for military purposes.[41]

Reports abound of an ongoing "shadow war" involving the United States and Israel against Iran. In this apparent conflict, alleged U.S.-Israel cyberattacks and Israel-sponsored assassinations of Iranian nuclear program principals are countered by alleged terrorist plots by Iran or its Lebanese

---

[37] Susser, "Strategic dilemmas," op. cit.

[38] Booth, op. cit.

[39] For background information on Iran and its nuclear program, see CRS Report RL32048, *Iran: U.S. Concerns and Policy Responses*, by Kenneth Katzman; CRS Report R40094, *Iran's Nuclear Program: Tehran's Compliance with International Obligations*, by Paul K. Kerr; and archived CRS Report R42443, *Israel: Possible Military Strike Against Iran's Nuclear Facilities*, coordinated by Jim Zanotti.

[40] Prospects that Iran's heavy-water reactor under construction in Arak might become operational as soon as 2014 could complicate efforts to compel Iran to comply with international demands to place verifiable limits on its production of fissile material that could be used for nuclear weapons—apparently adding to existing Israeli concerns regarding Iranian uranium enrichment. The reactor under construction in Arak has caused international concern because its spent fuel will contain plutonium well-suited for nuclear weapons. David Albright and Christina Walrond, "Update on the Arak Reactor," Institute for Science and International Security, July 15, 2013. However, for the plutonium to be usable, it must be separated from spent fuel—a procedure called "reprocessing." Iran has said that it will not engage in reprocessing and no evidence has emerged indicating that Iran is constructing a reprocessing facility. Iran has told the International Atomic Energy Agency (IAEA) that the reactor will operate under IAEA safeguards, is intended for the production of radio isotopes for medical purposes, and is scheduled to begin operating in 2014. Israeli observers have raised concerns that a military strike might not be feasible against the Arak reactor after it goes "hot" because of possible widespread environmental damage. Amos Yadlin and Avner Golov, "Iran's Plan B for the Bomb," *New York Times*, August 8, 2013.

[41] Transcript of remarks made by Netanyahu, Villa Taverna, Rome, Italy, October 23, 2013, available at http://www.state.gov/secretary/remarks/2013/10/215779.htm.

---

non-state ally Hezbollah against Israeli targets worldwide—including Bulgaria,[42] Cyprus, Georgia, Thailand, and India.

However, recent statements by Iran's new president, Hassan Rouhani, insisting that Iran is only seeking nuclear energy for peaceful purposes, along with statements from Supreme Leader Grand Ayatollah Ali Khamenei indicating possible greater openness to diplomacy on the nuclear issue,[43] may make an Israeli military strike against Iranian nuclear facilities unlikely in the near term as the United States and other international actors appear to seriously contemplate prospects for a negotiated solution. In his September 24 speech before the U.N. General Assembly, President Obama said that "statements made by our respective governments should offer the basis for a meaningful agreement.... But to succeed, conciliatory words will have to be matched by actions that are transparent and verifiable."[44]

It appears that Israel, in the words of one U.S. commentator, is concerned that the United States "will accept a nuclear agreement that leaves Iran closer to a bomb than the Israelis would like to see them, sacrificing Israeli security interests as understood in Jerusalem in order to keep the US out of a war."[45] In response to the overtures from Iran and the United States, Netanyahu has said:

> Like North Korea before it, Iran will try to remove sanctions by offering cosmetic concessions, while preserving its ability to rapidly build a nuclear weapon at a time of its choosing. Israel would welcome a genuine diplomatic solution that truly dismantles Iran's capacity to develop nuclear weapons. But we will not be fooled by half-measures that merely provide a smokescreen for Iran's continual pursuit of nuclear weapons. And the world should not be fooled either.[46]

Within this context, Israeli leaders have publicly hinted that absent a clear resolution of Iran's nuclear activity to their satisfaction, they may order the Israeli military to strike Iranian nuclear facilities.[47] Moreover, an Israeli commentator asserted in September 2013 that President Obama's rhetoric and action in connection with threats of U.S. military action in Syria called into question "the credibility of America's commitment" on the Iranian track, possibly influencing Netanyahu to think "in earnest once again that Israel might have to act on its own."[48]

For its part regarding the Iranian nuclear issue, Congress continues to consider tighter sanctions against Iran,[49] and many congressional leaders appear to be reluctant to consider loosening sanctions as part of a potential nuclear deal absent verifiable action by Iran in support of its diplomatic overtures.[50] Israel supports a robust U.S. and international sanctions regime as one

---

[42] Several reports identify Hezbollah as the perpetrator of the July 2012 suicide bus bombing in Burgas, Bulgaria that targeted an Israeli tourist group—killing six (including the Bulgarian driver) and injuring 32. Nicholas Kulish and Eric Schmitt, "Hezbollah Is Blamed for Attack on Israeli Tourists in Bulgaria," *New York Times*, July 19, 2012.

[43] Arash Karami, "Ayatollah Khamenei's 'Heroic Flexibility,'" *Al-Monitor Iran Pulse*, September 19, 2013.

[44] White House transcript of remarks by President Obama at the U.N. General Assembly in New York, September 24, 2013.

[45] Walter Russell Mead, "Threading the Needle," *blogs.the-american-interest.com*, October 25, 2013.

[46] Israel Prime Minister's Office, PM Netanyahu's Statement on the Opening of the UN General Assembly, September 24, 2013.

[47] "Israel can strike Iran nuclear targets alone, IDF head says," *Times of Israel*, April 16, 2013.

[48] Leslie Susser, "Decision Time," *Jerusalem Report*, September 23, 2013.

[49] For more information, see CRS Report RS20871, *Iran Sanctions*, by Kenneth Katzman.

[50] Jennifer Rubin, "Congress remains 'skeptical' on Iran," *washingtonpost.com*, October 25, 2013.

possible means of compelling Iran to make concessions. Additionally, the Senate voted 99-0 on May 22, 2013, to pass a resolution in support of potential Israeli military action against Iran's nuclear program. As passed, the resolution (S.Res. 65) included the following language, along with a clause explicitly stating that it would not be construed as authorization for the use of force or as a declaration of war:

> if the Government of Israel is compelled to take military action in legitimate self-defense against Iran's nuclear weapons program, the United States Government should stand with Israel and provide, in accordance with United States law and the constitutional responsibility of Congress to authorize the use of military force, diplomatic, military, and economic support to the Government of Israel in its defense of its territory, people, and existence.[51]

Syria[52]

The Syrian civil war has increasingly become a security challenge for Israel. Israel became militarily involved in early 2013 to a limited extent. This involvement began with some strikes to retaliate against instances of artillery fire on its positions in the Golan Heights.[53] Subsequently, in February and May 2013, Israel allegedly conducted at least three separate airstrikes to prevent the transfer of sophisticated missiles or anti-aircraft weapons from the Asad regime to Hezbollah. Then, in July 2013, reports indicated that Israel may have conducted another airstrike in the Syrian port city of Latakia against Russian-origin anti-ship missiles.[54]

Israel reportedly has shared intelligence with the United States regarding the Asad regime's alleged use of chemical weapons.[55] Following the apparent August 21 chemical weapons attack in greater Damascus, Israeli officials apparently viewed the question of potential international intervention as having implications for the credibility of the United States and U.S. allies in the region. Israeli Prime Minister Binyamin Netanyahu said, "Now the whole world is watching. Iran is watching and it wants to see what would be the reaction on the use of chemical weapons."[56] Yet, some accounts indicated that Israeli officials had "little desire to see [Asad] toppled," given what could follow, and were "wary of creating any perception that they [were] meddling in either American politics or the civil war in neighboring Syria."[57]

After prospects of an imminent U.S.-led military intervention faded in September 2013 with a Russian proposal for Syria to give up its chemical weapons under international auspices—an arrangement reportedly welcomed by Israeli officials—indications of Israel's public ambivalence regarding the outcome of Syria's civil war continued. Michael Oren, Israel's outgoing ambassador

---

[51] On March 5, 2013, Representative Paul Gosar introduced H.Res. 98, which, if passed, would state the House's full support for "Israel's lawful exercise of self-defense, including actions to halt Iranian aggression such as a strike against Iran's illegal nuclear program." To date, H.Res. 98 has at least 31 co-sponsors (all of whom are Republican).

[52] For background information on Syria, see CRS Report RL33487, *Armed Conflict in Syria: Background and U.S. Response*, by Jeremy M. Sharp and Christopher M. Blanchard; and CRS Report R43201, *Possible U.S. Intervention in Syria: Issues for Congress*, coordinated by Christopher M. Blanchard and Jeremy M. Sharp.

[53] Israeli officials have expressed concern about spillover threats to the Golan Heights border area. For basic information on the U.N. Disengagement Observer Force (UNDOF) that has monitored this area since the Israel-Syria cease-fire in 1974, see http://www.un.org/en/peacekeeping/missions/undof/facts.shtml.

[54] Michael R. Gordon, "Some Syria Missiles Eluded Israeli Strike, Officials Say," *New York Times*, July 31, 2013.

[55] See, e.g., Ronen Bergman, "The Spies Inside Damascus," *Foreign Policy*, September 19, 2013.

[56] Josef Federman, "With Eye on Iran, Israelis Seek US Action in Syria," *Associated Press*, September 2, 2013.

[57] Ibid.

---

to the United States, gave an interview in which he stated that Israel had "always preferred the bad guys who weren't backed by Iran to the bad guys who were backed by Iran," but Oren's interview was closely followed by a statement from Prime Minister Netanyahu's office saying that "Israel's policy has not changed, and we are not intervening in internal Syrian affairs."[58]

In an October briefing to the Knesset Foreign Affairs and Defense Committee, Israeli Defense Minister Moshe Ya'alon reportedly enunciated the following "red lines" regarding Syria:

> We will not allow the transfer of high-quality weapons from Syria to hostile forces, particularly Hezbollah. We will not allow the transfer of chemical weapons, which there has been no attempt so far to transfer. And certainly we will not tolerate any disruption of our sovereignty in the Golan Heights.[59]

Potential weapons transfers, such as a possible Russian delivery of sophisticated S-300 anti-aircraft systems to Syria, could increase the risks for Israel in launching strikes beyond its borders.

Egypt[60]

During and since Egypt's July 2013 military-guided ouster of formerly-elected president Muhammad Morsi—a Muslim Brotherhood figure—Egyptian forces have reportedly been very active in countering heightened militant activity in Sinai and along its border with the Gaza Strip, and in targeting Sinai-Gaza smuggling tunnels.[61] Significant deployments of manpower and weaponry, which have reportedly been approved by and coordinated with Israel pursuant to key provisions in the two countries' 1979 peace treaty, seem to have been part of larger Egyptian military efforts to counter militant Islamist and tribal groups.[62] Media reports indicate that Israel is seeking continued U.S. and international support for Egypt under its new government.[63] Some reports suggest that an Israeli drone may have carried out an August airstrike—in coordination with the Egyptian military—against a jihadist militant group in Sinai.[64]

A core Israeli dilemma is how to support a more robust Egyptian security presence in Sinai to improve order and counter terrorism, while ensuring that Egypt adheres to the limitations on military deployment that underpin its peace treaty with Israel. Addressing this dilemma appears to

---

[58] Barak Ravid, "Netanyahu's office denies Ambassador Oren's claim that Israel favors rebels in Syrian civil war," *haaretz.com*, September 17, 2013.

[59] "'Israel will not accept deal that allows Iran to enrich uranium,'" *israelhayom.com*, October 23, 2013.

[60] For background information on Egypt, see CRS Report RL33003, *Egypt: Background and U.S. Relations*, by Jeremy M. Sharp.

[61] Egypt's task appears to be complicated by Hamas's possible harboring in Gaza of some militants who operate in Sinai. See, e.g., Avi Issacharoff, "Egypt's ire raised as Hamas harbors Sinai jihadists," *Times of Israel*, August 22, 2013.

[62] Yossi Melman, "The Sinai Imbroglio," *Jerusalem Report*, August 12, 2013.

[63] Ran Dagoni, "Israel fears US may suspend Egyptian aid," *globes-online.com*, July 4, 2013.

[64] Isabel Kershner and Rick Gladstone, "Israel Strikes 2 Gaza Sites Hours Before Talks Start," *New York Times*, August 15, 2013; Adnan Abu Amer, "Hamas, Gaza's Armed Factions Struggle to Stay Out of Sinai Conflict," *Al-Monitor Palestine Pulse*, August 15, 2013. Various accounts suggest that either an Israeli drone or an Egyptian military helicopter was responsible for the strike. The jihadist group, Majlis Shura al Mujahedeen fi Aknaf Bayt al Maqdis, claims to have retaliated against the August 9 killing of four of its fighters by firing rockets toward the Israeli Red Sea port city of Eilat on August 13. Israeli officials stated that Israel's Iron Dome anti-rocket system intercepted a rocket.

---

have relevance to the treaty's long-term durability. An August 2012 Sinai-based attack on an Egyptian garrison and Israeli border checkpoints—a year after another deadly Sinai-based attack in Israel—highlighted the threat posed by various terrorist groups, including those with links to Palestinian Islamists and global jihadists.[65] Additional border incursions have subsequently occurred.

Rocket Threat from Lebanon and Gaza

Israel continues to face a rocket threat from the Gaza Strip/Sinai Peninsula (via Hamas and other militant groups) and Lebanon (via Hezbollah) that has expanded in geographical range in the past few years. Israel engaged in a weeklong conflict with Hamas and other Palestinian militants in November 2012, and the resulting Egyptian-mediated, U.S.-supported cease-fire has largely held. However, there has been little or no lasting progress in arresting the rocket threat or in negotiating an easing of Israel's perimeter of control in and around Gaza. Meanwhile, Israel continues to deploy and develop programs to defend against a wide variety of ranges of rockets and missiles.

The Palestinian Issue

At the same time, despite the renewal of direct Israel-PLO talks during the summer of 2013 there is little indication of progress toward a conflict-ending negotiated settlement between Israel and the Palestinians. Neither Israeli leaders, nor Fatah or Hamas leaders preoccupied with maintaining their domestic credibility and respective territorial fiefdoms in the West Bank and Gaza, appear disposed to make substantive compromises with one another. It is unclear to what extent stalemate on the Palestinian issue could worsen regional tensions and anti-Israel sentiment, or motivate greater international action seeking to establish Israeli legal and moral culpability for its treatment of Palestinians. Periodically recurring incidents of violence and vandalism involving Israelis (including West Bank settlers) who live and travel in close proximity to Palestinians highlight the difficulty Israeli authorities face both in restraining and protecting their citizens, and could contribute to future tensions.

Political figures from the Israeli left and center, as well as some U.S. and international commentators, continue to stress what they characterize as an urgent need for Israel to resolve its disputes with the Palestinians. Some analysts assert that Israeli leaders face a dilemma between democracy and demography.[66] Past prime ministers, including Yitzhak Rabin and Ehud Olmert, claimed that coming to an arrangement with the Palestinians on the West Bank and Gaza would be necessary in order to avoid the situation—otherwise probable within the next decade or two based on demographic trends—of Jews ruling as a numerical minority over a numerical majority of Arabs in historic Palestine. The concerns they enunciated focus on possible domestic and international pressure associated with these demographics, and a choice between giving up Jewish primacy or facing intensified accusations that Jewish rule in the areas of historic Palestine is undemocratic and contrary to the principle of self-determination. Some demographers have disputed the data underlying these concerns. Additionally, the apparent primacy of socioeconomic issues in the 2013 elections could signal that Israelis feel less urgency about the issue than in past years.

---

[65] Melman, "The Sinai Imbroglio," op. cit.

[66] Akiva Eldar, "Israel's New Politics and the Fate of Palestine," *The National Interest*, July/August 2012; Peter Beinart, *The Crisis of Zionism*, New York: Times Books, 2012.

Prime Minister Netanyahu has increasingly endorsed a two-state solution in public on demographic grounds, but such concerns appear to be less of a motivating factor for key members of the government such as Defense Minister Moshe Ya'alon[67] and Economy Minister Naftali Bennett. Some Israeli peace process opponents, including Deputy Defense Minister and Likud Party Central Committee Chair Danny Danon, have claimed that despite efforts Netanyahu might make to forward the process, his government will not allow it to proceed to completion.[68]

See "Peace Process Diplomacy" below for information and analysis on recent developments regarding the peace process, including regional factors.

Concerns Regarding International Isolation

Israel and many of its supporters have expressed concern about a sense of international isolation.[69] Israel's willingness to show flexibility regarding its security practices, negotiating demands, or diplomatic tactics may depend on whether its leaders believe that changes in their policies can change attitudes toward them. Some Israelis argue or imply that efforts to isolate them are led by implacable enemies determined to spread anti-Israel and anti-Semitic attitudes, and thus bear little or no relationship to Israel's policies.[70] Other Israelis assert a more direct relationship between Israeli policies, such as the construction of Jewish communities or "settlements" (the term used most commonly internationally) in the West Bank and East Jerusalem, and international attitudes toward Israel. This latter set routinely laments what they characterize as extreme approaches by their leaders toward charged issues like the Israeli-Palestinian conflict.[71]

Israel is likely to need U.S. help in improving or mitigating the damage done to various regional and international relationships, though even with this help, any repairing of relationships may be halting and reversible. U.S.-aided efforts by Israel to repair deteriorated relations with Turkey provide an example. During President Barack Obama's March 2013 visit to Israel, Prime Minister Netanyahu apologized via telephone to Turkish Prime Minister Recep Tayyip Erdogan for any operational mistakes by Israel during the Gaza flotilla incident of May 2010 "that might have led

---

[67] In a June 2012 interview, Ya'alon said, "We can live like this for another 100 years, too.... The demographic argument is a lie." Ari Shavit, "IDF chief of staff-turned-vice premier: 'We are not bluffing,'" *Ha'aretz Magazine*, June 14, 2012.

[68] Raphael Ahren, "Deputy defense minister: This government will block any two-state deal," *Times of Israel*, June 6, 2013; Nathan Jeffay, "Danny Danon, Hardline 'King' of Israel's Likud, Vows To Block Two-State Deal," *Jewish Daily Forward*, July 12, 2013. Former Israeli Prime Minister Ariel Sharon left the Likud Party in 2005 after Israel's withdrawal from the Gaza Strip led to intra-party contention. Netanyahu became the party's leader in Sharon's stead.

[69] Israel's president, Shimon Peres, and former prime ministers Ehud Olmert and Ehud Barak have reportedly warned that "unless the occupation of the bulk of the West Bank ends, or Palestinians in the West Bank are given full voting rights in Israel, the country will lose its claim to be a democracy. It will, says Mr. Peres, become a 'pariah', just as South Africa did. The BDS [boycott, divestment, and sanctions] campaign may thus, he implies, become unstoppable. Even the Americans might find it hard to go on backing Israel come hell or high water." "Could two become one?," *Economist*, March 16-22, 2013.

[70] See, e.g., Barry Rubin, "The Region: Is Israel losing support?," *jpost.com*, January 6, 2013.

[71] In response to Israel's announcement of plans to expand settlement construction in the West Bank and East Jerusalem following the United Nations General Assembly vote in November 2012 to change the observer status of "Palestine" (the PLO) within the U.N. system from that of an entity to a "non-member state," former Israeli prime minister Ehud Olmert was quoted as saying, "Netanyahu is isolating the State of Israel from [the] entire world in an unprecedented way, and we are going to pay a difficult price for this in every aspect of our lives." "Former PM Olmert: Netanyahu is isolating Israel from the rest of the world," *haaretz.com*, December 8, 2012.

---

to the loss of life or injury," and also agreed to conclude an agreement on "compensation/nonliability."[72] However, subsequent difficulties in concluding such an agreement have been compounded by a number of developments, including statements from Erdogan blaming Egypt's July 2013 military takeover on Israel, and media reports that surfaced in October 2013 alleging that in 2012 Turkey revealed to Iran the names of sources used by Israel's Mossad intelligence agency.[73] Debate persists on the extent to which Israel-Turkey rapprochement is likely, and on how it might take place.[74]

Key U.S. Policy Issues

Overview

On May 14, 1948, the United States became the first country to extend de facto recognition to the state of Israel. Over the years, despite occasional policy differences, the United States and Israel have maintained close bilateral ties based on common democratic values, religious affinities, and security interests. Relations have evolved through legislation; memoranda of understanding; economic, scientific, and military agreements; and trade. Congress provides military assistance to Israel and has enacted other legislation in explicit support of its security. Many analysts view these forms of support as pillars of a regional security order—largely based on varying types and levels of U.S. arms sales to Israel and Arab countries—that have discouraged the outbreak of major Arab-Israeli interstate conflict for nearly 40 years.[75]

Israeli officials closely monitor U.S. actions and consult with U.S. counterparts in apparent efforts to gauge and influence the nature and scope of future U.S. engagement on and commitment to regional issues that implicate Israel's security. In consequence of possible Israeli concerns about these issues and about potential changes in levels of U.S. interest and influence in the region, Israeli leaders and their supporters may actively try to persuade U.S. decision makers both that

- Israel's security and the broader stability of the region continue to be critically important for U.S. interests; and

- Israel has substantial and multifaceted worth as a U.S. ally beyond temporary geopolitical considerations and shared ideals and values.[76]

These efforts would seek to perpetuate and bolster the already strong popular and official U.S. commitment to Israel's security. According to one U.S. commentator, American Israel Public

---

[72] Summary of conversation between Netanyahu and Erdogan from Israeli Prime Minister's Office website, March 22, 2013. The May 2010 Gaza flotilla incident involved the boarding in international waters by Israeli commandos of a ship that was commissioned by a Turkish Islamist non-governmental organization to carry goods to the Israeli-blockaded Gaza Strip. Under disputed circumstances, the commandos reportedly killed eight Turks and an American of Turkish ancestry and injured several others.

[73] David Ignatius, "Turkey blows Israel's cover for Iranian spy ring," *Washington Post*, October 16, 2013.

[74] Continuing Israeli restrictions and limitations on the passage of people and goods to and from Gaza's sea coast and its land borders with Israel remain a potential sticking point. State Department transcript of remarks by Secretary of State John Kerry and Turkish Foreign Minister Ahmet Davutoglu, Ciragan Palace, Istanbul, Turkey, April 7, 2013.

[75] Malka, op. cit., pp. 93-94.

[76] See, e.g., Michael Eisenstadt and David Pollock, *Asset Test: How the United States Benefits from Its Alliance with Israel*, Washington Institute for Near East Policy, September 2012.

Affairs Committee (AIPAC) president Michael Kassen has deplored what he describes as "the 'growing allure of isolationism' in America, which is another way of saying that Israel, among other nations, may command less deference and interest among a new and younger generation of legislators."[77]

Israel-sponsored efforts to emphasize its importance to the United States also may aim to minimize possible demands by U.S. policymakers for Israel to compensate the United States for a potentially greater commitment to Israel in response to regional challenges.[78] Expectations among some U.S. officials could include greater Israeli deference to and coordination with the United States on regional military action and on diplomacy with Palestinians. This could fuel or intensify U.S.-Israel disagreement over how Israel might continue its traditional prerogative of "defending itself, by itself," while also receiving external assistance.

The U.S.-Israel discourse on key issues affecting Israel's security apparently features points of agreement on overall goals but differences in priorities. A basic dynamic in bilateral discussions during President Obama's and Prime Minister Netanyahu's terms in office appears to have been an Israeli preference to press for international action on threats from Iran, and a U.S. emphasis on achieving progress on the Palestinian issue.[79] Although the recent resumption of Israeli-Palestinian direct talks may reflect some movement by Israel toward the U.S. perspective, it is also possible that Netanyahu's willingness to countenance action on the Palestinian front is largely calculated to elicit reciprocation from the United States on the Iranian nuclear issue.[80]

Security Cooperation[81]

Background

Strong bilateral relations have fueled and reinforced significant U.S.-Israel cooperation on defense, including military aid, arms sales, joint exercises, and information sharing. It has also included periodic U.S.-Israel governmental and industrial cooperation in developing military technology.

U.S. military aid has helped transform Israel's armed forces into one of the most technologically sophisticated militaries in the world. This aid for Israel has been designed to maintain Israel's "qualitative military edge" (QME) over neighboring militaries, since Israel must rely on better equipment and training to compensate for a manpower deficit in any potential regional conflict. U.S. military aid, a portion of which may be spent on procurement from Israeli defense

---

[77] Jacob Heilbrunn, "Israel's Fraying Image," *National Interest*, May/June 2013.

[78] According to one report, some U.S. military officers and analysts, including "senior Pentagon officials, generals and independent defense strategists," weigh the "direct military benefits the United States receives from its partnership with Israel ... against the geopolitical costs the relationship imposes on Washington in its dealings with the broader Arab and Muslim world; some suggest a net negative outcome for Washington in the equation." Nathan Guttman, "Israel Is Strategic Asset After All," *Jewish Daily Forward*, November 18, 2011.

[79] Ben Caspit, "What Really Happened Between Netanyahu and Obama," *Al-Monitor Israel Pulse*, April 11, 2013.

[80] See, e.g., Susser, "Decision Time," op. cit.; Aaron David Miller, "What makes John Kerry think he can secure peace in Israel?," *Washington Post*, July 26, 2013.

[81] The Jewish Virtual Library maintains a page that contains hyperlinked documents, speeches, and reports under the heading "U.S.-Israel Relations: Strategic & Military Cooperation," available at http://www.jewishvirtuallibrary.org/jsource/US-Israel/strattoc html.

---

companies, also has helped Israel build a domestic defense industry, and Israel in turn ranks as one of the top 10 exporters of arms worldwide.

On November 30, 1981, then U.S. Secretary of Defense Caspar Weinberger and Israeli Defense Minister Ariel Sharon signed a memorandum of understanding (MOU) establishing a framework for consultation and cooperation to enhance the national security of both countries. In November 1983, the two sides formed a Joint Political Military Group (JPMG) to implement provisions of the MOU. Joint air and sea military exercises began in June 1984, and the United States has constructed facilities to stockpile military equipment in Israel. In 1987, Israel was designated a "major non-NATO ally" by the Reagan Administration, and in 1988, under the terms of Section 517 of the Foreign Assistance Act of 1961, as amended, Congress codified this status, affording Israel preferential treatment in bidding for U.S. defense contracts and expanding its access to weapons systems at lower prices. In 2001, an annual interagency strategic dialogue, including representatives of diplomatic, defense, and intelligence establishments, was created to discuss long-term issues. This dialogue was halted in 2003 over bilateral tensions related to Israeli arms sales to China (see "Israeli Arms Sales to Other Countries" below), but resumed in 2005.

On May 6, 1986, Israel and the United States signed an MOU—the contents of which are classified—for Israeli participation in the Strategic Defense Initiative (SDI/"Star Wars"), under which U.S.-Israel co-development of the Arrow ballistic missile defense system has proceeded, as discussed below. In 1998, another U.S.-Israel MOU referred to growing regional threats from ballistic missiles. This MOU said that "In the event of such a threat, the United States Government would consult promptly with the Government of Israel with respect to what support, diplomatic or otherwise, or assistance, it can lend to Israel."

Security cooperation extends to cooperation in countering terrorism. The Implementing Recommendations of the 9/11 Commission Act of 2007 (P.L. 110-53, enacted on August 3, 2007) recognizes Israel as a potential research partner for the Department of Homeland Security.

Congress and the President enacted the U.S.-Israel Enhanced Security Cooperation Act (P.L. 112-150) in July 2012. The act contains non-binding "sense of Congress" language focusing largely on several possible avenues of cooperation discussed below, including providing Excess Defense Articles; boosting operational, intelligence, and political-military coordination; expediting specific types of arms sales (such as F-35 fighter aircraft, refueling tankers, and "bunker buster" munitions); and additional aid for Israel's Iron Dome anti-rocket system and U.S.-Israel cooperative missile defense programs. The act also extended deadlines for Israel to access U.S. military stockpiles.

Pending Legislation – U.S.-Israel Strategic Partnership Act of 2013

In early March 2013, slightly differing versions of a U.S.-Israel Strategic Partnership Act of 2013 were introduced in the House (H.R. 938) and the Senate (S. 462) with bipartisan co-sponsors.[82] Both versions refer to Israel as a "major strategic partner" of the United States—a designation whose meaning has not been further defined in U.S. law or by the executive branch—and contain various other provisions that encourage continued and expanded U.S.-Israel cooperation in a number of areas. Both versions also would extend the war reserves stockpile authority[83] for Israel

---

[82] To date, H.R. 938 has at least 345 sponsors, and S. 462 has at least 53.

[83] For information on the war reserves stockpile authority, under which the United States maintains munitions (continued...)

through FY2015, and would seek to have the executive branch give Israel the same Strategic Trade Authorization (STA) licensing exception for certain munitions and dual-use items that 36 other countries currently have.[84]

Preserving Israel's Qualitative Military Edge (QME)

Since the late 1970s, successive Administrations have argued that U.S. arms sales are an important mechanism for addressing the security concerns of Israel and other regional countries. During this period, some Members of Congress have argued that sales of sophisticated weaponry to Arab countries may erode Israel's QME over its neighbors. However, successive Administrations have maintained that Arab countries are too dependent on U.S. training, spare parts, and support to be in a position to use sophisticated U.S.-made arms against the United States, Israel, or any other U.S. ally in a sustained campaign. Arab critics routinely charge that Israeli officials exaggerate the threat they pose. Ironically, the threat of a nuclear-armed Iran, though it has partially aligned Israeli and Sunni Arab interests in deterring a shared rival, may be exacerbating Israeli fears of a deteriorated QME, as Saudi Arabia and other Gulf states dramatically increase defense procurements from U.S. and other foreign suppliers.

In 2008, Congress enacted legislation requiring that any proposed U.S. arms sale to "any country in the Middle East other than Israel" must include a notification to Congress with a "determination that the sale or export of such would not adversely affect Israel's qualitative military edge over military threats to Israel."[85] In parallel with this legal requirement, U.S. and Israeli officials continually signal their shared understanding of the U.S. commitment to maintaining Israel's QME. However, the codified definition focuses on preventing arms sales to potential regional Israeli adversaries based on a calculation of conventional military threats. It is unclear whether calls for revisiting this definition or rethinking its implementation may arise in light of the evolving nature of potential regional threats to Israel's security.

Additionally, what might constitute a legally defined adverse effect to QME is not clarified in U.S. legislation. After the passage of the 2008 legislation, a bilateral QME working group was created allowing Israel to argue its case against proposed U.S. arms sales in the region.[86] However, absent legislative clarification, the legality of future U.S. arms sales to other regional

---

(...continued)

stockpiles for its own use and for Israel's use in emergency situations with U.S. permission, see CRS Report RL33222, *U.S. Foreign Aid to Israel* , by Jeremy M. Sharp

[84] For information on the STA licensing exception, see Export Control Reform Initiative Factsheet #4: License Exception "Strategic Trade Authorization" (STA). Available at: http://new.export.gov/cms_files/ECR%20Factsheet%204%20-%20STA_Latest_eg_main_047475.pdf. Israel, along with seven other countries, currently has a more limited form of the STA licensing exception.

[85] §36(h) of the Arms Export Control Act, which contains the "qualitative military edge" requirement, was added by §201(d) of the Naval Vessel Transfer Act of 2008 (P.L. 110-429). The act defines QME as "the ability to counter and defeat any credible conventional military threat from any individual state or possible coalition of states or from non-state actors, while sustaining minimal damages and casualties, through the use of superior military means, possessed in sufficient quantity, including weapons, command, control, communication, intelligence, surveillance, and reconnaissance capabilities that in their technical characteristics are superior in capability to those of such other individual or possible coalition of states or non-state actors."

[86] Barbara Opall-Rome, "Israeli Brass Decry U.S. Arms Sales to Arab States," *Defense News*, January 23, 2012. According to this article, the U.S. side of the working group is led by the Undersecretary of Defense for Policy and Assistant Secretary of State for Political-Military Affairs, while the Israeli side is led by the Defense Ministry's policy chief and the Israel Defense Forces director of planning.

---

aid recipients, partners, or allies—including Egypt, Saudi Arabia, Jordan, Lebanon, and Iraq—could become increasingly subject to challenge both by Israeli officials feeling heightened sensitivity to regional threats and by sympathetic U.S. policymakers.

U.S. Security Guarantees?

Although the United States and Israel do not have a mutual defense treaty or agreement that provides formal U.S. security guarantees,[87] successive Administrations have either stated or implied that the United States would help provide for Israel's defense in the context of discussing specific threats, such as from Iran.[88] Both houses of Congress routinely introduce and pass resolutions supporting Israel's right to defend itself and U.S. efforts to bolster Israel's capacity for self-defense. Some resolutions have included language that could imply support for more active U.S. measures to defend Israel. For example, H.Res. 523 and H.Con.Res. 21, both of which overwhelmingly passed the House (in 2005 and 2007, respectively) and addressed a possible Iranian threat, also both reasserted the "commitment of the United States to defend the right of Israel to exist as a free and democratic state."[89] Additionally, as mentioned above, S.Res. 65, which the Senate passed in May 2013, stated that the United States should provide "diplomatic, military, and economic support to the Government of Israel in its defense of its territory, people, and existence" in connection with certain specified contingencies relating to Iran's nuclear program.

A former Israeli deputy national security advisor has written about potential benefits and drawbacks for Israel of more formal U.S. security guarantees for Israel, including a possible "nuclear umbrella." A 2006 article that this former official co-authored on a potential Iranian threat said:

> Such an arrangement would seem to be a "no-brainer" for Israel. Yet Jerusalem might in fact be quite reluctant to conclude one. This, for three primary reasons, each deeply entrenched in Israel's national security thinking. First, it would fear a loss of freedom of action, due to the contractual requirement to consult on the means of addressing the threat. Second, it would be concerned lest the US demand that Israel divulge and even forego its independent capabilities. And third, it might worry that the US would not live up to its nuclear commitments, much as NATO allies feared during the Cold War.[90]

---

[87] The United States and Israel do, however, have a Mutual Defense Assistance Agreement (TIAS 2675, dated July 23, 1952) in effect regarding the provision of U.S. military equipment to Israel (see "End-Use Monitoring"), and have entered into a range of stand-alone agreements, memoranda of understanding, and other arrangements varying in their formality.

[88] President Obama, in a February 5, 2012, NBC interview, said while responding to questions regarding a possible Israeli military strike against Iranian nuclear facilities: "I will say that we have closer military and intelligence consultation between our two countries than we ever have. And my number one priority continues to be the security of the United States, but also the security of Israel." In a March 2006 speech against the backdrop of Iran's hostile rhetoric toward Israel and pursuit of a nuclear program, President George W. Bush said, "I made it clear, I'll make it clear again, that we will use military might to protect our ally Israel." Seymour M. Hersh, "The Iran Plans," *New Yorker*, April 17, 2006.

[89] Additionally, in response to Iraqi Scud missile attacks on Israel during the 1991 Gulf War, both the House (H.Con.Res. 41) and Senate (S.Con.Res. 4) unanimously passed January 1991 resolutions "reaffirming America's continued commitment" to provide Israel with the means to maintain its freedom and security.

[90] Richard N. Rosecrance and Chuck Freilich, "Confronting Iran: A US Security Guarantee for Israel?," *bitterlemons-international.org*, July 6, 2006. See also Chuck Freilich, *Speaking About the Unspeakable: U.S.-Israeli Dialogue on Iran's Nuclear Program*, Washington Institute for Near East Policy, PolicyFocus #77, December 2007; Malka, op. cit., (continued...)

Perhaps at least partly due to some of the reasons this former Israeli official outlines, U.S. Administrations and Congress have supported Israel's ability to defend itself by embracing and even codifying the concept of helping maintain Israel's "qualitative military edge" (QME) over regional threats, as discussed above.

U.S. Aid and Arms Sales to Israel

Specific figures and comprehensive detail regarding various aspects of U.S. aid and arms sales to Israel are discussed in CRS Report RL33222, *U.S. Foreign Aid to Israel* , by Jeremy M. Sharp. This includes information on conditions that generally allow Israel to use its military aid earlier and more flexibly than other countries, and on the effects of budget sequestration regarding various forms of assistance to Israel.

Israel is the largest cumulative recipient of U.S. foreign assistance since World War II. From 1976 to 2004, Israel was the largest annual recipient of U.S. foreign assistance, but has since been supplanted—first by Iraq, then by Afghanistan. Since 1985, the United States has provided approximately $3 billion in grants annually to Israel. In the past, Israel received significant economic assistance, but now almost all U.S. bilateral aid to Israel is in the form of Foreign Military Financing (FMF). U.S. FMF to Israel represents approximately one half of total FMF and 20% of Israel's defense budget. The remaining five years of a 10-year bilateral memorandum of understanding commits the United States to $3.1 billion annually from FY2014 to FY2018, subject to congressional appropriations. Israel uses approximately 75% of its FMF to purchase arms from the United States, in addition to receiving U.S. Excess Defense Articles (EDA). Congress routinely provides hundreds of millions of dollars in additional annual assistance for the Israel's Iron Dome anti-rocket system[91] and joint U.S.-Israel missile defense programs such as Arrow and David's Sling.[92]

During an April 2013 visit to Israel, Secretary of Defense Chuck Hagel confirmed arms sales worth a total of $10 billion to Israel, Saudi Arabia, and the United Arab Emirates.[93] The deal, which most observers assert is intended to counter Iranian regional influence, would reportedly include new-generation KC-135 refueling tankers that could increase Israeli long-range strike capabilities, such as for military action against Iranian nuclear facilities.[94] In a report before the deal's official announcement, a *New York Times* article stated that "Congressional officials said

---

(...continued)

pp. 84-89.

[91] Reports based on Israeli military sources indicate that initial uses of Iron Dome in 2011 and 2012, including during the November 2012 Israel-Gaza conflict, showed a high rate of success—possibly around 80%—in intercepting short-range rockets fired from Gaza. It is unknown if the United States or another third party has independently verified Israeli claims, and analysts have debated the claims' validity. Although Iron Dome is costly in comparison with the Gaza-based rockets it has intercepted, analysts debate whether the system's cost-effectiveness is better measured by armament attrition or by comparing the system's costs with estimates of damage that would likely occur in its absence. See, e.g., Philip Giraldi, "Is Iron Dome the Maginot Line?," *theamericanconservative.com*, December 3, 2012; Matthew Fargo, "Iron Dome – A Watershed for Missile Defense?," *csis.org/blog*, December 3, 2012. For more information, see CRS Report RL33222, *U.S. Foreign Aid to Israel* , by Jeremy M. Sharp.

[92] For one analysis of Iron Dome and its possible implications for U.S. and Israeli missile defense efforts, see Peter Dombrowski, *et al.*, "Demystifying Iron Dome," *National Interest*, July-August 2013.

[93] David Alexander, "Arms deal with Middle East allies signal to Iran: Hagel," *Reuters*, April 21, 2013.

[94] Thom Shanker, "Arms Deal with Israel and 2 Arab Nations Is Near," *New York Times*, April 19, 2013.

---

members were seeking assurances that the package was in keeping with American policy to guarantee Israel's 'qualitative military edge' while not recklessly emboldening Israeli hawks."[95]

The United States also generally provides some annual American Schools and Hospitals Abroad (ASHA) funding and funding to Israel for migration assistance. Loan guarantees, arguably a form of indirect aid, also remain available to Israel through FY2015 under the U.S.-Israel Enhanced Security Cooperation Act (P.L. 112-150).

Table 3. U.S. Bilateral Aid to Israel

(historical $ in millions)

Year	Total	Military Grant	Economic Grant	Immig. Grant	ASHA	All other
1949-1996	68,030.9	29,014.9	23,122.4	868.9	121.4	14,903.3
1997	3,132.1	1,800.0	1,200.0	80.0	2.1	50.0
1998	3,080.0	1,800.0	1,200.0	80.0	—	—
1999	3,010.0	1,860.0	1,080.0	70.0	—	—
2000	4,131.85	3,120.0	949.1	60.0	2.75	—
2001	2,876.05	1,975.6	838.2	60.0	2.25	—
2002	2,850.65	2,040.0	720.0	60.0	2.65	28.0
2003	3,745.15	3,086.4	596.1	59.6	3.05	—
2004	2,687.25	2,147.3	477.2	49.7	3.15	9.9
2005	2,612.15	2,202.2	357.0	50.0	2.95	—
2006	2,534.5	2,257.0	237.0	40.0	—	0.5
2007	2,503.15	2,340.0	120.0	40.0	2.95	0.2
2008	2,423.9	2,380.0	—	40.0	3.90	—
2009	2,583.9	2,550.0	—	30.0	3.90	—
2010	2,803.8	2,775.0	—	25.0	3.80	—
2011	3,029.22	3,000.0	—	25.0	4.225	—
2012	3,098.0	3,075.0	—	20.0	3.00	—
2013	3,115.0 (Before Sequestration)	3,100.0	—	15.0	—	—
2014	3,115.0	3,100.0	—	15.0	—	—

[95] Ibid. Section 1266 of the version of the FY2014 National Defense Authorization Act passed by the House in June 2013 (H.R. 1960) contains a clause stating that "It is the policy of the United States to take all necessary steps to ensure that Israel possesses and maintains an independent capability to remove existential threats to its security and defend its vital national interests." The same section would require the President, within 90 days of the Act's enactment, to provide a report to pertinent committees that does the following: (1) identifies all aerial refueling platforms, bunker-buster munitions, and other capabilities and platforms that would contribute significantly to the maintenance by Israel of a robust independent capability to remove existential security threats, including nuclear and ballistic missile facilities in Iran, and defend its vital national interests; (2) assesses the availability for sale or transfer of items necessary to acquire the capabilities and platforms described in paragraph (1) as well as the legal authorities available for making such transfers; and (3) describes the steps the President is taking to immediately transfer such items.

Year	Total	Military Grant	Economic Grant	Immig. Grant	ASHA	All other
Request						
Total	118,247.57	70,523.4	30,897.0	1,673.2	162.075	14,991.9

Notes: FY2000 military grants include $1.2 billion for the Wye agreement and $1.92 billion in annual military aid. For information on U.S. loan guarantees to Israel, see CRS Report RL33222, *U.S. Foreign Aid to Israel*, by Jeremy M. Sharp.

Table 4. Defense Budget Appropriations for U.S.-Israeli Missile Defense: FY2006-FY2014 Request

(historical $ in millions)

Fiscal Year	Arrow II	Arrow III (High Altitude)	David's Sling (Short-Range)	Iron Dome	Total
FY2006	122.866	—	10.0	—	132.866
FY2007	117.494	—	20.4	—	137.894
FY2008	98.572	20.0	37.0	—	155.572
FY2009	74.342	30.0	72.895	—	177.237
FY2010	72.306	50.036	80.092	—	202.434
FY2011	66.427	58.966	84.722	205.0	415.115
FY2012	58.955	66.220	110.525	70.0[a]	305.700
FY2013 Before Sequestration	44.365	74.692	149.679	211.0	479.736
FY2014 Request	10.663	52.607	32.512	220.0	315.782

a. These funds were not appropriated by Congress, but reprogrammed by the Obama Administration from other Department of Defense accounts.

Israeli-Palestinian Issues

For historical background on these issues, see CRS Report RL34074, *The Palestinians: Background and U.S. Relations*, by Jim Zanotti.

Peace Process Diplomacy

Background

The internationally mandated land-for-peace framework that has undergirded U.S. policy since the June 1967 Arab-Israeli War presupposes broad Arab acceptance of any final-status Israeli-Palestinian agreement, and, more fundamentally, Arab acceptance of Israel. Israelis insist that their security needs must be met for them to be willing to relinquish West Bank land in a negotiated two-state solution with the Palestinians. However, Israeli leaders appear to have become increasingly concerned—given ongoing Arab political change—that they cannot count on future positive ties even with states such as Egypt and Jordan.[96] This assessment has likely led Israel to perceive greater risks in a potential land-for-peace deal, perhaps due to a calculation that continued possession of territory may be a more reliable guarantor of security than an agreement with one or more Arab entities.

For their part, Palestinian leaders and Arab state rulers may find it harder to move toward formal peace with Israel if they become more accountable to public opinion focused on Israel and its indicia of control in the West Bank, Gaza, and Jerusalem. Formally, the League of Arab States (Arab League) remains committed to "land for peace," as reflected in the 2002 Arab Peace Initiative.[97]

The United States, together with the other members of the international Quartet (the European Union, the United Nations Secretary-General's office, and Russia), continues to advocate for Israeli-Palestinian talks aimed at a peace deal under the framework initially established by the Oslo agreements of the 1990s. During the first two years of President Obama's and Prime Minister Netanyahu's time in office, attempts by Palestinians to link a meaningful resumption of negotiations to a freeze in Israeli settlement construction beyond the Green Line (the armistice line that divided Israel from the West Bank prior to the 1967 Arab-Israeli War)—claiming inspiration from Obama's public call for this freeze in 2009—were unsuccessful.[98]

During the next two years, PLO Chairman Mahmoud Abbas opted to pursue initiatives outside of the negotiating process at the United Nations and U.N.-related agencies. These initiatives were aimed at increasing the international legitimacy of Palestinian claims of statehood in the West Bank and Gaza. On November 29, 2012, the U.N. General Assembly (UNGA) adopted Resolution 67/19, changing the permanent observer status of the PLO (recognized as "Palestine" within the U.N. system) from an "entity" to a "non-member state."[99] This took place a year after the PLO gained admission in November 2011 to the U.N. Educational, Scientific and Cultural Organization (UNESCO).[100] The change that Resolution 67/19 made to the PLO's U.N.

---

[96] Egypt and Jordan were routinely held out as examples showing that even if making peace with Israel was unpopular with the countries' populations, their autocratic or monarchical leaders could normalize and maintain relations with Israel without significantly losing their capacity or legitimacy to rule.

[97] The Arab Peace Initiative offers a comprehensive Arab peace with Israel if Israel were to withdraw fully from the territories it occupied in 1967, agree to the establishment of a Palestinian state with a capital in East Jerusalem, and provide for the "[a]chievement of a just solution to the Palestinian Refugee problem in accordance with UN General Assembly Resolution 194." The initiative was proposed by then Crown Prince (now King) Abdullah of Saudi Arabia, adopted by the 22-member Arab League (which includes the PLO), and later accepted by the 56-member Organization of the Islamic Conference (now the Organization of Islamic Cooperation) at its 2005 Mecca summit. The text of the initiative is available at http://www.bitterlemons.org/docs/summit.html.

[98] Netanyahu accepted the idea of a two-state solution in principle, but insisted that any Palestinian state would need to be demilitarized and remain subject to indefinite Israeli control of its airspace, the electromagnetic spectrum used for telecommunications, and the Jordan Valley. President Obama's May 2011 speeches calling for renewed Israeli-Palestinian negotiations focused on the issues of borders and security parameters. Netanyahu complained that Obama's proposal to use the Green Line as the reference point for border negotiations did not properly take into account historical Israeli security concerns regarding defensibility of territory.

[99] 138 member states voted in favor of Resolution 67/19, nine voted against (including the United States and Israel), and 41 abstained. The PLO has had permanent observer status at the United Nations since 1974. "Palestine" maintains many of the capacities it had as an observer entity—including participation in General Assembly debates and the ability to co-sponsor draft resolutions and decisions related to proceedings on Palestinian and Middle East issues. However, it is not a member of the United Nations, and does not have the right to vote or to call for a vote in the General Assembly.

[100] However, the PLO's fall 2011 application to obtain membership in the United Nations was unsuccessful. U.N. (continued...)

---

permanent observer status is largely symbolic. However, it may increase the probability that the Palestinians and other international actors could take future steps—particularly in the International Criminal Court (ICC)—toward legal action against Israelis for alleged violations of international laws and norms regarding the treatment of people and property in the West Bank and Gaza.[101]

Resumption of Direct Negotiations

Shortly after beginning his second term, President Obama traveled to Israel in March 2013 and told the Israeli people that "this is precisely the time to respond to the wave of revolution [in the region] with a resolve and commitment for peace."[102] After Secretary of State Kerry made several trips to the region, he convened talks in July between Israeli and Palestine Liberation Organization (PLO) negotiators in Washington, DC, to discuss a framework for final-status negotiations on issues of Israeli-Palestinian dispute. The discussions that subsequently began in Jerusalem in mid-August at the envoy/negotiator level are the first direct Israel-PLO negotiations since September 2010. Also in July, Kerry appointed Martin Indyk, a former U.S. Ambassador to Israel and Clinton Administration official, as U.S. Special Envoy for Israeli-Palestinian Negotiations.[103] President Obama has endorsed the talks' resumption, and identified them in his September 24, 2013, U.N. General Assembly address as one of two specific short-term priorities of U.S. diplomacy (the other being the Iranian nuclear issue).[104] Yet, it is unclear to what extent Obama plans to play a direct role. On September 25, Kerry said that he and President Obama would consult with Israeli Prime Minister Binyamin Netanyahu and PLO Chairman/Palestinian Authority (PA) President Mahmoud Abbas as "we think appropriate" to move the process forward:

(...continued)

Security Council, "Report of the Committee on the Admission of New Members concerning the application of Palestine for admission to membership in the United Nations," S/2011/705, November 11, 2011.

[101] An April 2012 opinion by the ICC's Office of the Prosecutor, which determined that there was no basis for it to consider a declaration of consent by "Palestine" to ICC jurisdiction in the West Bank and Gaza, appeared to rule that guidance from the U.N. General Assembly would be decisive in determining whether the PLO or Palestinian Authority had competence as a state to consent to ICC jurisdiction. International Criminal Court, Office of the Prosecutor, "Situation in Palestine," April 3, 2012. Some analyses assert, however, that legal ambiguities remain. See, e.g., John Cerone, "Legal Implications of the UN General Assembly Vote to Accord Palestine the Status of Observer State," *insights*, American Society of International Law, December 7, 2012. For more information on the ICC, see CRS Report R41116, *The International Criminal Court (ICC): Jurisdiction, Extradition, and U.S. Policy*, by Matthew C. Weed.

[102] White House transcript of remarks by President Barack Obama, Jerusalem International Convention Center, March 21, 2013.

[103] The British-born, Australian-raised Indyk has served twice as Ambassador to Israel (1995-1997 and 2000-2001), and also served during the Clinton Administration as a senior Middle East official on the National Security Council and in the State Department. He was closely involved with the Oslo-era negotiations coordinated by then U.S. envoy Dennis Ross. Kerry has appointed his longtime aide Frank Lowenstein as Indyk's deputy and as a senior advisor to Kerry. Former Senator George Mitchell served as Special Envoy for Middle East Peace from 2009 (shortly after President Obama's inauguration) until his 2011 resignation, and was followed by David Hale, a career diplomat with considerable Middle East experience.

[104] White House transcript of remarks by President Obama at the U.N. General Assembly in New York, September 24, 2013.

Purposefully, we want the Palestinians and Israelis to meet together, work this through, build trust, build relationship. But at the same time, we are there to facilitate, to help if there needs to be a bridging proposal to work on the way forward.[105]

Prior to the renewed talks, Israel's coalition government approved the eventual release of 104 Palestinian prisoners, and both sides reportedly agreed to give the talks at least nine months—probably making it less likely that the PLO would, during that time, pursue international initiatives aimed at strengthening claims of Palestinian statehood. Thus far, Israel has coupled its releases of Palestinian prisoners (it has released 52 of the 104) with announcements of plans relating to the construction of settlement housing in the West Bank and East Jerusalem, presumably to placate Israeli nationalist constituencies on the right of the political spectrum who strongly oppose prisoner releases both in principle and in practice.[106] In response to a press conference question on the subject of Israel's settlement announcements, Secretary Kerry characterized all settlements as "illegitimate," but also stated:

> Prime Minister Netanyahu was completely upfront with me and with President Abbas that he would be announcing some additional building that would take place in places that will not affect the peace map, that will not have any impact on the capacity to have a peace agreement. That means that it is building within the so-called blocs in areas that many people make a presumption—obviously not some Palestinians or others—will be part of Israel in the future. He has specifically agreed not to disturb what might be the potential for peace going forward. Now, we still believe it would be better not to be doing it, but there are realities within life in Israel that also have to be taken into account here going forward.[107]

Speculation continues over the extent to which U.S. officials may seek to secure agreement:

- by Israel to the use of the Green Line as the reference point for a West Bank-Gaza border negotiation involving possible land swaps; and

- by the PLO to accept the "Jewish character" of Israel, as well as constraints on most Palestinian refugees from the 1947-1948 Arab-Israeli war from eventually returning to the areas (now within Israel) from which they fled and/or were driven.

Both Netanyahu and Abbas may have resumed the peace process partly in order to avoid blame for talks otherwise failing to relaunch. Though Secretary Kerry has indicated that the parties have agreed to discuss all issues of dispute, and has stated that the goal is a final-status agreement, not an interim agreement, remarks he made in August 2013 indicate that he may anticipate prioritizing resolution on borders, security arrangements, and West Bank settlements in some way before resolving other matters.[108]

---

[105] Transcript of remarks by Secretary of State John Kerry, "Remarks at the Meeting of the Ad Hoc Liaison Committee," United Nations, New York, September 25, 2013.

[106] See, e.g., Jodi Rudoren, "1,500 Units to Be Added in Settlement, Israel Says," *New York Times*, October 30, 2013.

[107] Transcript of remarks by Secretary of State John Kerry, "Remarks with Brazilian Foreign Minister Antonio de Aguiar Patriota After Their Meeting," Itamaraty Palace, Brasilia, Brazil, August 13, 2013.

[108] Ibid.

Israeli Perspectives

Israeli willingness to engage might also be linked to concerns about international "isolation," particularly in light of a July directive by the European Union (EU) prohibiting EU funding to Israeli organizations operating in West Bank, East Jerusalem, or Golan Heights settlements. As discussed earlier in this report (see "The Palestinian Issue"), Netanyahu has been increasingly indicating a preference for Israel to pursue a two-state solution rather than for it to risk having binationalism imposed upon Israel at some point in the future.[109] Netanyahu might be legally required to call a referendum[110] to overcome widespread opposition to peace negotiations from key elements within his government—including his own Likud party and the pro-settler party Ha'bayit Ha'Yehudi (Jewish Home). Additionally, in October 2013, the Knesset's Ministerial Committee on Legislation approved the Knesset's consideration of a bill that would require two-thirds majority Knesset approval before Israel could negotiate concessions on Jerusalem.[111]

Such opposition may at least partly reflect objections by many Israelis to relinquishing West Bank territory on religious and ideological grounds and/or due to security concerns. Reportedly, a U.S. team led by retired Marine General John R. Allen[112] is working to convince Israeli officials that scenarios exist—possibly featuring U.S. and other international participation—for maintaining security following a potential Israeli military drawdown from parts of the West Bank. It is unclear how effective General Allen's efforts might be in persuading Israelis, given past examples where Israeli withdrawals from southern Lebanon and the Gaza Strip led to periodic attacks and persistent threats from militants, and in light of turmoil in Syria and Egypt. This could be complicated by an apparent uptick since late August 2013 in Palestinian unrest in East Jerusalem and the West Bank, including some violent Israeli and Palestinian deaths.[113]

Palestinian Perspectives

Although Abbas also faces significant domestic opposition and skepticism regarding renewed talks, some obstacles to PLO engagement appear to have been somewhat alleviated or at least temporarily removed. First, concerns about conceding territory appear to have been mitigated by statements of support from Arab states. In late April 2013, then Prime Minister Sheikh Hamad bin Jassim al Thani of Qatar said during a visit to Washington, DC, with other Arab League officials that "comparable and mutual[ly] agreed minor" land swaps could be one aspect of a conflict-ending agreement.[114]

---

[109] Considerable public debate in Israel takes place regarding Jewish-Arab demographics in Israel-West Bank-Gaza Strip; their potential domestic, regional, and international implications; and possible Israeli options. See, e.g., Leslie Susser, "The Right Touts a One-State Solution," *Jerusalem Report*, July 29, 2013.

[110] In late July, the cabinet approved a bill that, upon Knesset passage, would establish a Basic Law requiring a popular referendum to approve any peace agreement under which Israel would withdraw from land it has militarily controlled since the 1967 Arab-Israeli war.

[111] Jonathan Lis, "Ministers back bill requiring 66% Knesset majority to negotiate Jerusalem status," *haaretz.com*, October 20, 2013. Israeli Justice Minister and peace process negotiator Tzipi Livni has appealed the ministerial committee's decision.

[112] General Allen commanded all U.S. and U.S.-allied forces in Afghanistan from 2011 to 2013.

[113] Amos Harel, "Attacks in the West Bank: Signs of a brewing intifada?," *haaretz.com*, October 11, 2013.

[114] State Department transcript of remarks by al Thani, Washington, DC, April 29, 2013. Arab League officials restated their openness to land swaps in a July statement released in Amman, Jordan.

Second, although Hamas's control of Gaza and the group's considerable Palestinian base of support continue to challenge Abbas's claim to be a credible "partner for peace," Hamas's regional political support appears to have declined. First, at the end of 2011, Syria's civil war distanced Hamas from Iran and the Asad regime. Then, during the summer of 2013, political transitions in Egypt and Qatar disempowered Hamas-friendly leaders in those countries, and Egypt's military operations in Sinai and increased criticism of alleged Hamas links to Sinai-based militants have disrupted aspects of Hamas's rule in Gaza, including the revenues it receives from smuggling tunnels.[115]

Jerusalem

Israel annexed East Jerusalem (which includes the walled Old City, with its Temple Mount/Haram al Sharif and Western Wall, and most of the surrounding "historic basin") and some of its immediate West Bank vicinity in 1967—shortly after occupying these areas militarily in the June 1967 Arab-Israeli War. In doing so, Israel joined these newly occupied areas,[116] which featured a predominantly Arab population, to the predominantly Jewish western part of the city it had controlled since 1948. Israel proclaimed this entire area to be Israel's eternal, undivided capital.[117] Polls indicate that a large majority of Israelis believe that a united Jerusalem is their capital and support Jewish residential construction of neighborhoods (the Israeli term) or settlements (the general internationally used term) within that part of Jerusalem that is east of the Green Line and within the Israeli-drawn municipal borders.[118] Israel's annexation of areas beyond the Green Line is generally not internationally recognized.

Successive U.S. Administrations of both political parties since 1948 have maintained that the fate of Jerusalem is to be decided by negotiations and have discouraged the parties from taking actions that could prejudice the final outcome of those negotiations. Moreover, the Palestinians envisage East Jerusalem as the capital of their future state. However, the House of Representatives passed H.Con.Res. 60 in June 1997, and the Senate passed S.Con.Res. 21 in May 1997. Both resolutions called on the Clinton Administration to affirm that Jerusalem must remain the undivided capital of Israel.

A related issue is the possible future relocation of the U.S. embassy from Tel Aviv to Jerusalem. Proponents argue that Israel is the only country where a U.S. embassy is not in the capital identified by the host country, that Israel's claim to West Jerusalem—proposed site of an embassy—is unquestioned, and/or that Palestinians must be disabused of their hope for a capital in Jerusalem. Opponents say such a move would undermine prospects for Israeli-Palestinian peace and U.S. credibility with Palestinians and in the Muslim world, and could prejudge the final status of the city. The Jerusalem Embassy Act of 1995 (P.L. 104-45) provided for the embassy's relocation by May 31, 1999, but granted the President authority, in the national security interest, to suspend limitations on State Department expenditures that would be imposed if the embassy

---

[115] Avi Issacharoff, "Hamas, circa 2013, is in a lot of trouble," *Times of Israel*, October 29, 2013.

[116] Jordan had occupied these areas militarily since 1948, and unilaterally annexed them and the entire West Bank in 1950. It only ceded its claims to the Palestine Liberation Organization (PLO) in 1988.

[117] In 1980, under the first Likud Party government, the Israeli Knesset passed the Basic Law: Jerusalem—Capital of Israel, which declares "Jerusalem, complete and united, is the capital of Israel." See http://www.mfa.gov.il for the complete text of the Basic Law. Israel had first declared Jerusalem to be its capital in 1950.

[118] "Poll: Most Israelis Support East Jerusalem Construction," *Ynetnews.com*, March 22, 2010.

---

did not open. Presidents Clinton, Bush, and Obama have consistently suspended these spending limitations, and the embassy's status has remained unchanged.

The State Department Authorization Act for FY2002-FY2003 (P.L. 107-228) urged the President to begin relocating the U.S. embassy "immediately." The act also sought to (1) prohibit the use of appropriated funds for the operation of U.S. diplomatic facilities in Jerusalem unless such facilities were overseen by the U.S. ambassador to Israel; and (2) allow Israel to be recorded as the place of birth of U.S. citizens born in Jerusalem. When signing the act into law, President George W. Bush wrote in an accompanying "signing statement" that the various provisions on Jerusalem would, "if construed as mandatory … impermissibly interfere with the president's constitutional authority to conduct the nation's foreign affairs." The State Department declared, "our view of Jerusalem is unchanged. Jerusalem is a permanent status issue to be negotiated between the parties."

The case of *Zivotofsky v. Clinton*,[119] remanded by the Supreme Court in March 2012 for further action in lower federal courts, could decide or have implications for Congress's constitutional authority on questions relating to the status of Jerusalem and could influence its future ability to direct the executive branch in its conduct of foreign affairs more broadly. The case involves a U.S. citizen who was born in Jerusalem, and whose parents are suing on his behalf to have the State Department reflect Israel as his birthplace on his passport pursuant to P.L. 107-228. On remand, the U.S. Court of Appeals for the District of Columbia Circuit found in July 2013 that the "President's power to recognize foreign nations is exclusive and trumps Congress's authority to regulate passports."[120] The Supreme Court might reconsider the case on appeal.

Over successive Congresses, including the 113th, various Members have periodically introduced substantially similar versions of a Jerusalem Embassy and Recognition Act (e.g., H.R. 104, H.R. 252, and S. 604) or thematically related bills or resolutions (e.g., H.R. 2846 and H.Con.Res. 48). Such bills and resolutions seek the embassy's relocation and would remove or advocate for the removal of the President's authority to suspend the State Department expenditure limitations cited above.

Settlements

Israel has approximately 139 residential communities (known internationally and by significant segments of Israeli society as "settlements"), approximately 105 settlement outposts unauthorized under Israeli law, and other military and civilian land-use sites in the West Bank. In addition, depending on how one defines what constitutes a separate neighborhood or settlement in East Jerusalem, Israeli authorities and Jewish Israeli citizens have established roughly between 14 and 17 main residential areas there. Approximately 300,000 Israelis live in West Bank settlements, with roughly 200,000 more in East Jerusalem.[121] All of these residential communities are located in areas that the Palestinians view as part of their future state. The first settlements were

---

[119] *Zivotofsky v. Clinton*, U.S. Supreme Court Docket No. 10-699, March 26, 2012.

[120] CRS Legal Sidebar, Jennifer K. Elsea, Legislative Attorney, "Congress Can't Dictate Jerusalem Policy," August 12, 2013, available at http://www.crs.gov/LegalSidebar/details.aspx?ID=612&Source=search. The D.C. Circuit's July 2013 opinion is available at http://www.cadc.uscourts.gov/internet/opinions nsf/C8DC59BCC7D10E6D85257BB10051786D/$file/07-5347-1447974.pdf.

[121] These figures and additional data on settlements and outposts are available at http://www fmep.org/settlement_info.

---

constructed following the 1967 war, and were initially justified as directly associated with Israel's military occupation of the West Bank. Major residential settlement building began in the late 1970s with the advent of the pro-settler Gush Emunim ("Bloc of the Faithful") movement and the 1977 electoral victory of Menachem Begin and the Likud Party. Existing settlements were expanded and new ones established throughout the 1990s and 2000s despite the advent of the Madrid-Oslo peace process with the Palestinians. Israelis who defend the settlements' legitimacy generally use some combination of legal, historical, strategic, nationalistic, or religious justifications.[122]

The international community generally considers Israeli construction on territory beyond the Green Line to be illegal.[123] Israel retains military control over the West Bank and has largely completed a separation barrier[124] on West Bank territory that in some places corresponds with the Green Line but in others goes significantly beyond it. The barrier is intended to separate Israelis and Palestinians and prevent terrorists from entering Israel. Palestinians object to the barrier being built on their territory because it cuts Palestinians off from East Jerusalem and, in some places, bisects their landholdings and communities. It also is seen by many as an Israeli device to unilaterally determine borders between Israel and a future Palestinian state.

U.S. policy on settlements has varied since 1967. Until the 1980s, multiple Administrations either stated or implied that settlements were "contrary to international law," with President Carter's Secretary of State Cyrus Vance stating explicitly that settlements were "illegal" in 1980.[125] President Reagan later stated that settlements were "not illegal," but "ill-advised" and "unnecessarily provocative." Since then, the executive branch has generally refrained from pronouncements on the settlements' legality.[126] A common U.S. stance has been that settlements are an "obstacle to peace." Loan guarantees to Israel currently authorized by U.S. law are subject to possible reduction by an amount equal to the amount Israel spends on settlements in the occupied territories. The executive branch made its most recent reduction in FY2005.[127]

An April 2004 letter from President George W. Bush to then Israeli Prime Minister Ariel Sharon explicitly acknowledged that "in light of new realities on the ground, including already existing major Israeli populations (sic) centers, it is unrealistic to expect that the outcome of final status negotiations will be a full and complete return to the armistice lines of 1949." Partly because of

---

[122] For more information on the history of the settlements and their impact on Israeli society, see Idith Zertal and Akiva Eldar, *Lords of the Land: The War for Israel's Settlements in the Occupied Territories, 1967-2007*, New York: Nation Books, 2007; Gershom Gorenberg, *The Accidental Empire: Israel and the Birth of the Settlements, 1967-1977*, New York: Times Books, 2006.

[123] The most cited international law pertaining to Israeli settlements is the Fourth Geneva Convention, Part III, Section III, Article 49 *Relative to the Protection of Civilian Persons in Time of War*, August 12, 1949, which states in its last sentence, "The Occupying Power shall not deport or transfer parts of its own civilian population into the territory it occupies." Israel insists that the West Bank does not fall under the international law definition of "occupied territory," but is rather "disputed territory" because the previous occupying power (Jordan) did not have an internationally recognized claim to it, and given the demise of the Ottoman Empire at the end of World War I and the end of the British Mandate in 1948, no international actor has superior legal claim to it.

[124] Israelis and Palestinians generally use very different terminology to describe the barrier. Many Israelis call it the "security barrier" or "security fence," while most Palestinians refer to it as the "wall" or "apartheid wall."

[125] Daniel Kurtzer, "Do Settlements Matter? An American Perspective," *Middle East Policy*, vol. 16, issue 3, Fall 2009.

[126] Nicholas Rostow, "Are the Settlements Illegal?," *The American Interest*, March/April 2010.

[127] For more information on this issue, see CRS Report RL33222, *U.S. Foreign Aid to Israel* , by Jeremy M. Sharp.

---

such statements from U.S. policymakers, Arab critics routinely charge that U.S. support of Israel indirectly supports settlement activity.

Upon taking office, in the context of its attempts to restart the peace process between Israelis and Palestinians, the Obama Administration called for Israel to totally freeze all settlement activity, including in East Jerusalem. In his speech in Cairo in May 2009, President Obama said, "The United States does not accept the legitimacy of continued Israeli settlements. This construction violates previous agreements and undermines efforts to achieve peace. It is time for these settlements to stop."[128] PLO leaders followed suit and made a settlement freeze a precondition for their return to the peace talks. Israel responded with a partial 10-month moratorium, but tentative efforts to restart negotiations did not take hold during that time. In February 2011, the United States vetoed a draft U.N. Security Council resolution that would have characterized Israeli settlements in the West Bank and East Jerusalem as illegal. All other 14 members of the Council, including the United Kingdom, France, and Germany, voted for the draft resolution. Susan Rice, then the U.S. Permanent Representative to the United Nations, clarified that the Administration still opposed settlement construction as illegitimate and at cross-purposes with peace efforts.[129]

Given the structure of Israeli society and politics, it may be difficult to impose an external restraint on settlement activity. Settlers affect the political and diplomatic calculus through the following means:

(1) influence over key voting blocs in Israel's coalition-based parliamentary system (although they do not all share the same ideology or interests, settlers constitute about 6% of the Israeli population);

(2) renegade actions to foment public protest and even violence;[130] and

(3) what they represent for some symbolically, emotionally, and even spiritually as guardians of the last frontier for a country whose founding and initial survival depended on pioneering spirit in the face of adversity.

The Netanyahu government's periodic announcement of new plans for settlement construction, possible consideration of legalizing some settlement outposts, approval of subsidies and loans for some settlers, and repeated insistence that outside actors will not dictate Israeli policy on this subject appears to demonstrate the government's sensitivity to these domestic concerns.[131] Some

---

[128] U.S. and Israeli leaders publicly differed on whether Obama's expectations of Israel contradicted statements that the George W. Bush Administration had made. Some Israeli officials and former Bush Administration officials said that the United States and Israel had reached an unwritten understanding that "Israel could add homes in settlements it expected to keep [once a final resolution with the Palestinians was reached], as long as the construction was dictated by market demand, not subsidies." Glenn Kessler and Howard Schneider, "U.S. Presses Israel to End Expansion," *Washington Post*, May 24, 2009. This article quotes former Bush Administration deputy national security advisor Elliott Abrams as saying that the United States and Israel reached "something of an understanding." The accounts of former Bush Administration officials diverge in their characterization of U.S.-Israel talks on the subject, but the Obama Administration has insisted that if understandings ever existed, it is not bound by them. Ethan Bronner, "Israelis Say Bush Agreed to West Bank Growth," *New York Times*, June 3, 2009.

[129] "United States vetoes Security Council resolution on Israeli settlements," UN News Centre, February 18, 2011.

[130] Mark Weiss, "Settlers Destroy Trees on West Bank," *Irish Times*, July 22, 2009: "Militant settlers, who often act independently, in defiance of the official settler leadership, confirmed that a 'price tag' policy exists under which revenge attacks will be carried out against Palestinians every time the government acts to remove outposts."

[131] Joel Greenberg, "Netanyahu strengthens his base within Likud," *Washington Post*, February 2, 2011.

Israelis caution that the demand to provide security to settlers and their infrastructure and transportation links to Israel could perpetuate Israeli military control in the West Bank even if other rationales for maintaining such control eventually recede. Protecting settlers is made more difficult and manpower-intensive by some settlers' provocations of Palestinian West Bank residents and Israeli military authorities. The government complied in 2012 with rulings by Israel's Supreme Court requiring it to dismantle two outposts. It has sought to placate settler opposition to dismantlement by relocating the displaced outpost residents within the boundaries of settlements permitted under Israeli law.[132]

Sensitive Defense Technology and Intelligence Issues

Arms sales, information sharing, and co-development of technology between the United States and Israel raises questions about what Israel might do with capabilities or information it acquires. The sale of U.S. defense articles or services to Israel and all other foreign countries is authorized subject to the provisions of the Arms Export Control Act (AECA) (see §40A of P.L. 90-629, as amended)[133] and the regulations promulgated to implement it. Section 3 of the AECA stipulates that in order to remain eligible to purchase U.S. defense articles, training, and services, foreign governments must agree not to use purchased items and/or training for purposes other than those permitted by the act, or to transfer them to third-party countries (except under certain specifically enunciated conditions), without the prior consent of the President.

Israeli Arms Sales to Other Countries

Israel is a major arms exporter—with India, China, and Russia among its customers or past customers.[134] The United States and Israel have regularly discussed Israel's sale of sensitive security equipment and technology to various countries, especially China.[135] In 2003, Israel's agreement to upgrade radar-seeking Harpy Killer drones that it sold to China in 1999 dismayed the Department of Defense (DOD). DOD retaliated by suspending its joint strategic dialogue with Israel and its technological cooperation with the Israel Air Force on the F-35 Joint Strike Fighter (JSF) aircraft and several other programs, among other measures.

On August 17, 2005, DOD and the Israeli Ministry of Defense issued a joint press statement reporting that they had signed an understanding "designed to remedy problems of the past that seriously affected the technology security relationship and to restore confidence in the technology

---

[132] Joel Greenberg, "Israeli settlers evacuated from West Bank outpost following court order," *Washington Post*, September 2, 2012.

[133] 22 U.S.C. §2785.

[134] Other customers for Israeli arms include Germany, Spain, France, Canada, Australia, Turkey, Singapore, Brazil, Italy, the Netherlands, Poland, Finland, Azerbaijan, and Romania. Israel is also reportedly seeking to expand arms exports to Latin America.

[135] Office of Naval Intelligence, *Worldwide Challenges to Naval Strike Warfare*, 1996. The 1997 edition of this report said that the design for China's J-10 fighter (also known as the F-10—the designation used in the report) "had been undertaken with substantial direct assistance, primarily from Israel and Russia, and with indirect assistance through access to U.S. technologies." ONI, *Worldwide Challenges to Naval Strike Warfare*, 1997. See also Robert Hewson, "Chinese J-10 'benefited from the Lavi project,'" *Jane's Defence Weekly*, May 16, 2008; Duncan L. Clarke and Robert J. Johnston, "U.S. Dual-Use Exports to China, Chinese Behavior, and the Israel Factor: Effective Controls?" *Asian Survey*, Vol. 39, No. 2, March-April 1999. The Lavi fighter (roughly comparable to the U.S. F-16) was developed in Israel during the 1980s with approximately $1.5 billion in U.S. assistance, but did not get past the prototype stage.

---

security area."[136] Thereafter, the U.S.-Israel joint strategic dialogue resumed. Sources have reported that this understanding has given the United States de facto veto power over Israeli third-party arms sales that the United States deems harmful to its national security interests.[137]

End-Use Monitoring

Sales of U.S. defense articles and services to Israel are made subject to the terms of both the AECA and the July 23, 1952 Mutual Defense Assistance Agreement between the United States and Israel (TIAS 2675). The 1952 agreement states:

> The Government of Israel assures the United States Government that such equipment, materials, or services as may be acquired from the United States ... are required for and will be used solely to maintain its internal security, its legitimate self-defense ... and that it will not undertake any act of aggression against any other state.

Past Administrations have acknowledged that some Israeli uses of U.S. defense articles may have gone beyond the requirements under the AECA and the 1952 agreement that Israel use such articles for self-defense and internal security purposes. These past Administrations have transmitted reports to Congress stating that "substantial violations" of agreements between the United States and Israel regarding arms sales "may have occurred." The most recent report of this type was transmitted in January 2007 in relation to concerns about Israel's use of U.S.-supplied cluster munitions during military operations against Hezbollah in Lebanon during 2006.[138] Other examples include findings issued in 1978, 1979, and 1982 with regard to Israel's military operations in Lebanon and Israel's air strike on Iraq's nuclear reactor complex at Osirak in 1981. The Reagan Administration suspended the delivery of cluster munitions to Israel from 1982 to 1988 based on concerns about their use in Lebanon. The Reagan Administration also briefly delayed a scheduled shipment of F-15 and F-16 aircraft to Israel following Israel's 1981 strike on Iraq. If Israel takes future action with U.S. defense articles to preempt perceived security threats, allegations of AECA violations could follow.[139]

---

[136] "U.S. Israel Agree to Consult on Future Israeli Weapons Sales -Nations Affirm Joint Commitment to Address Global Security Challenges," U.S. State Department Press Release, August 17, 2005.

[137] "U.S. OKs Israel-China Spy Sat Deal," *DefenseNews.com*, October 12, 2007. This article quotes a U.S. official as saying, "We don't officially acknowledge our supervisory role or our de facto veto right over their exports.... It's a matter of courtesy to our Israeli friends, who are very serious about their sovereignty and in guarding their reputation on the world market."

[138] Sean McCormack, U.S. Department of State Spokesman, Daily Press Briefing, Washington, DC, January 29, 2007. The Consolidated Appropriations Act, 2008 (P.L. 110-161) significantly restricted the export of U.S.-manufactured cluster munitions. Restrictions on cluster munitions exports have been carried forward to apply to appropriations in subsequent years as well. Since 2008, Israel has been acquiring domestically manufactured cluster munitions.

[139] Some Palestinian groups and other Arab and international governments, along with at least one Member of Congress, have characterized Israeli military operations against Palestinians (such as Israel's 2008-2009 Operation Cast Lead, which was directed against Hamas in the Gaza Strip) as acts of aggression. During the 111th Congress, the Senate and the House overwhelmingly passed resolutions during the week of January 5, 2009 in connection with Operation Cast Lead that supported Israel's right to defend itself (S.Res. 10 and H.Res. 34). Representative Dennis Kucinich, however, submitted a letter to then Secretary of State Condoleezza Rice arguing that "Israel's most recent attacks neither further internal security nor do they constitute 'legitimate' acts of self-defense." Office of Representative Dennis J. Kucinich, "Press Release: Israel May Be in Violation of Arms Export Control Act," January 6, 2009.

Espionage-Related Cases

In the past 25 years, there have been at least three cases in which U.S. government employees were convicted of disclosing classified information to Israel or of conspiracy to act as an Israeli agent. The most prominent is that of Jonathan Pollard, who pled guilty in 1986 with his then wife Anne to selling classified documents to Israel. Israel granted Pollard—who is serving a life sentence in U.S. federal prison—citizenship in 1996 and, in 1998, acknowledged that Pollard had been its agent. Prime Minister Netanyahu and several of his predecessors have unsuccessfully petitioned various Presidents to pardon Pollard.[140]

Israel's Nuclear Status and Non-Proliferation[141]

Consensus among media and expert reports is that Israel possesses an arsenal of 80 to 200 nuclear weapons.[142] The United States has countenanced Israel's nuclear ambiguity since September 1969, when Israeli Prime Minister Golda Meir and U.S. President Richard Nixon reportedly reached an accord whereby both sides agreed never to acknowledge Israel's nuclear arsenal in public.[143]

Israel's ambiguous nuclear status is viewed by some members of the international community as an obstacle to advancing non-proliferation objectives. The 1995 Non-Proliferation Treaty (NPT) Review Conference adopted a resolution that called for "all States in the Middle East to take practical steps" toward establishing "an effectively verifiable Middle East zone free of weapons of mass destruction, nuclear, chemical and biological, and their delivery systems." The Obama Administration has stated its support for the goal of a nuclear-weapon-free zone in the Middle East. Israel is not an NPT state, nor has it ratified the Chemical Weapons Convention (CWC), though it signed the CWC in 1993.

Events during 2013 concerning Iran and Syria have re-focused international attention on Israel's presumed but undeclared nuclear and chemical weapons arsenals.[144] On September 26, Iranian President Hassan Rouhani called for Israel to become a signatory to the Nuclear Non-Proliferation Treaty (NPT) under the rationale that no exceptions to nuclear nonproliferation in the Middle East should be countenanced by the international community.[145] Media reports in late October indicated that Israeli officials may be discreetly discussing with Arab and Iranian

---

[140] The second case is that of Department of Defense analyst Lawrence Franklin, who pled guilty in 2006 to disclosing classified information to an Israeli diplomat and to two lobbyists from the American Israel Public Affairs Committee (AIPAC). The third case is that of Ben-Ami Kadish, who had worked at the U.S. Army's Armament Research, Development, and Engineering Center in Dover, New Jersey. Kadish pled guilty in 2009 to one count of conspiracy to act as an unregistered agent of Israel.

[141] For information on Israel's nuclear activities, see CRS Report R40439, *Nuclear Weapons R&D Organizations in Nine Nations*, coordinated by Jonathan E. Medalia.

[142] See footnote 35.

[143] Eli Lake, "Secret U.S.-Israel Nuclear Accord in Jeopardy," *Washington Times*, May 6, 2009.

[144] Barak Ravid, "Israel opts to stay vague on chemical arms policy in wake of Syria disarmament," *haaretz.com*, October 31, 2013.

[145] Matthew Lee and Lara Jakes, "Iran's Rouhani Calls On Israel To Sign 1979 Nuclear Non-Proliferation Treaty," *Associated Press*, September 26, 2013.

representatives the possibility of participating in a committee to discuss demilitarizing weapons of mass destruction throughout the region.[146]

Bilateral Trade Issues

The United States is Israel's largest single-country trading partner,[147] and—according to data from the U.S. International Trade Commission—Israel is the United States's 26th-largest trading partner.[148] The two countries concluded a Free Trade Agreement (FTA) in 1985, and all customs duties between the two trading partners have since been eliminated. The FTA includes provisions that protect both countries' more sensitive agricultural sub-sectors with non-tariff barriers, including import bans, quotas, and fees. Israeli exports to the United States have grown since the FTA became effective. Qualified Industrial Zones (QIZs) in Jordan and Egypt are considered part of the U.S.-Israel free trade area. In 2012, Israel imported $14.3 billion in goods from and exported $22.1 billion in goods to the United States.[149] The United States and Israel have launched several programs to stimulate Israeli industrial and scientific research, for which Congress has authorized and appropriated funds on several occasions.[150]

The "Special 301" provisions of the Trade Act of 1974, as amended, require the U.S. Trade Representative (USTR) to identify countries which deny adequate and effective protection of intellectual property rights (IPR). In April 2005, the USTR elevated Israel from its "Watch List" to its "Priority Watch List" because it had an "inadequate data protection regime" and intended to pass legislation to reduce patent term extensions. The USTR has retained Israel on the Priority Watch List in subsequent years, including in 2012, when it was one of 13 countries on the list.[151]

Pending Visa Waiver Legislation

Both the House and the Senate versions of the U.S.-Israel Strategic Partnership Act of 2013 (H.R. 938 and S. 462, respectively) encourage Israel's inclusion in the U.S. visa waiver program.[152] The

---

[146] Sarah Leah Lawrent and M. Miskin, "Israeli, Arab Reps Meet to Discuss WMD-Free Middle East," *israelnationalnews.com*, October 31, 2013.

[147] According to a document entitled "Israel: EU Bilateral Trade and Trade with the World" generated by the European Commission's Directorate General for Trade on May 23, 2013, the countries of the European Union account for 31.6% of Israel's total trade volume, while the United States accounts for 20.1%.

[148] Statistics on Israel's status relative to other U.S. trading partners compiled by the U.S. International Trade Commission, available at http://dataweb.usitc.gov/SCRIPTS/cy_m3_run.asp.

[149] Statistics compiled by Foreign Trade Division, U.S. Census Bureau, available at http://www.census.gov/foreign-trade/balance/c5081 html.

[150] CRS Report RL33222, *U.S. Foreign Aid to Israel*, by Jeremy M. Sharp.

[151] The other 12 are Algeria, Argentina, Canada, Chile, China, India, Indonesia, Pakistan, Russia, Thailand, Ukraine, and Venezuela. *2012 Special 301 Report*, available at http://www.ustr.gov. According to this report, the United States and Israel reached an Understanding on Intellectual Property Rights, "which concerns several longstanding issues regarding Israel's regime for pharmaceutical products, on February 18, 2010. As part of the Understanding, Israel committed to strengthen its laws on protection of pharmaceutical test data and patent term extension, and to publish patent applications promptly after the expiration of a period of eighteen months from the time an application is filed. The Understanding provided, among other things, that Israel would submit legislation regarding these matters within 180 days of the conclusion of the Understanding. The United States agreed to move Israel to the Watch List once Israel submitted appropriate legislation to the Knesset, and to remove Israel from the Special 301 Watch List once the Government enacted legislation implemented Israel's obligations fully."

[152] For more information, see CRS Report RL32221, *Visa Waiver Program*, by Alison Siskin.

Senate version would amend the Immigration and Nationality Act (8 U.S.C. §1187(c)(2)) to exempt Israel from a requirement that links program country eligibility to a specific maximum rate of past nonimmigrant visa refusals. S. 462 also might provide an exemption for Israel from the general legal requirement that a country provide reciprocal visa-free travel privileges to U.S. citizens if the Secretary of State certifies that Israel has made "every reasonable effort, without jeopardizing the security of the State of Israel, to ensure that reciprocal travel privileges are extended to all United States citizens."

The possibility of an exemption for Israel on the reciprocity requirement has reportedly "drawn criticism from lawmakers, Arab-American groups and some Jewish critics, who say it would validate Israel's practice of profiling U.S. citizens of Arab, Muslim and Palestinian extraction and often denying them entry to the country on unspecified security grounds."[153] Senator Barbara Boxer, the bill's sponsor, has been cited as arguing that the provision in question would "give the United States leverage to pressure Israel" to stop the reported differential treatment of U.S. citizens based on ethnic background.[154] H.R. 938 would not provide visa waiver exemptions for Israel, but would instead simply state that Israel should be designated a visa waiver program country when it satisfies the requirements for inclusion. The visa waiver provision in S. 462 is substantially similar to stand-alone legislation on possible Israeli participation in the visa waiver program that was introduced earlier in 2013 in both the House (H.R. 300) and the Senate (S. 266).

---

[153] Jonathan Broder, "AIPAC-Backed Israel Bill Stalls Over Visa Waiver Provision," *cq.com*, April 29, 2013. See also Yousef Munayyer, "A Lopsided U.S. Visa-Waiver," *New York Times*, October 28, 2013.

[154] Broder, op. cit.

Appendix A. U.S.-Based Interest Groups Relating to Israel

Selected groups actively interested in Israel and the peace process are noted below with links to their websites for information on their policy positions.

American Israel Public Affairs Committee: http://www.aipac.org

American Jewish Committee: http://www.ajc.org

American Jewish Congress: http://www.ajcongress.org

Americans for Peace Now: http://www.peacenow.org

Anti-Defamation League: http://www.adl.org

Conference of Presidents of Major Jewish Organizations: http://www.conferenceofpresidents.org

Foundation for Middle East Peace: http://www.fmep.org

Hadassah (The Women's Zionist Organization of America, Inc.): http://www.hadassah.org

Israel Bonds: http://www.israelbonds.com

Israel Institute: http://www.israelinstitute.org

The Israel Project: http://www.theisraelproject.org

Israel Policy Forum: http://www.israelpolicyforum.org

J Street: http://jstreet.org

Jewish National Fund: http://www.jnf.org

Jewish Policy Center: http://www.jewishpolicycenter.org

New Israel Fund: http://www.nif.org

S. Daniel Abraham Center for Middle East Peace: http://www.centerpeace.org

The Telos Group: http://www.telosgroup.org

United Israel Appeal: http://www.jewishfederations.org/united-israel-appeal.aspx

Zionist Organization of America: http://www.zoa.org

Appendix B. Electoral Lists Represented in Knesset

Likud (Consolidation)/ **Yisrael Beiteinu** (Israel Is Our Home)	Likud: Israel's historical repository of right-of-center nationalist ideology; skeptical of territorial compromise; has also championed free-market reforms. *Leader: Binyamin Netanyahu*
	Yisrael Beiteinu: Pro-secular, right-of-center nationalist party with base of support among Russian speakers from former Soviet Union. *Leader: Avigdor Lieberman*
Yesh Atid (There Is a Future)	New pro-secular, centrist party focusing largely on socioeconomic issues, including conscription of Haredim and easing middle class burdens. *Leader: Yair Lapid*
Avoda (Labor)	Israel's historical repository of social democratic, left-of-center, pro-secular Zionist ideology; although associated with efforts to end Israel's responsibility for Palestinians in West Bank and Gaza, has campaigned this cycle largely on socioeconomic issues. *Leader: Shelly Yachimovich*
Ha'bayit Ha'Yehudi (The Jewish Home)	Right-of-center nationalist coalition with base of support among Ashkenazi Orthodox Jews; includes core constituencies supporting West Bank settlements and annexation. *Leader: Naftali Bennett*
Shas	Mizrahi ultra-orthodox (Haredi) party guided by Rabbi Ovadia Yosef; favors welfare and education funds in support of Haredi lifestyle; opposes conscription of Haredim and compromise with Palestinians on control over Jerusalem. *Leaders: Eli Yishai, Aryeh Deri, and Ariel Atias*
Ha'tnua (The Movement)	New pro-secular, centrist party focusing on ending Israel's responsibility for Palestinians in West Bank and Gaza, preferably via negotiation, and preserving international support for Israel. *Leader: Tzipi Livni*
United Torah Judaism (UTJ)	Ashkenazi Haredi coalition (Agudat Yisrael and Degel Ha'torah); favors welfare and education funds in support of Haredi lifestyle; opposes conscription of Haredim; generally seeks greater application of Jewish law. *Leaders: Yaakov Litzman and Moshe Gafni*
Hadash (Democratic Front for Peace and Equality)	Israeli Arab-Jewish socialist party; supports complete Israeli withdrawal to 1949-1967 armistice lines, creation of a Palestinian state, and religion/state separation. *Leader: Mohammed Barakeh*
Ra'am (United Arab List)/ **Ta'al** (Arab Movement for Renewal)	Israeli Arab coalition with base of support among Islamists and Bedouins; supports creation of Palestinian state along 1949-1967 armistice lines. *Leaders: Ibrahim Sarsur and Ahmad Tibi*
Balad (National Democratic Assembly/"Country")	Israeli Arab party; supports a two-state solution. *Leader: Jamal Zahalka*
Meretz	Left-of-center, pro-secular Zionist party that supports initiatives for social justice and for peace with the Palestinians. *Leader: Zahava Gal-On*
Kadima (Forward)	Centrist party offshoot from Likud espousing similar principles to Ha'tnua; top vote-getter in 2006 and 2009 elections. *Leader: Shaul Mofaz*

Author Contact Information

Jim Zanotti
Specialist in Middle Eastern Affairs
jzanotti@crs.loc.gov, 7-1441